THE HARD TIMES
COOKBOOK

First published in 2009 by
Liberties Press
Guinness Enterprise Centre | Taylor's Lane | Dublin 8
www.LibertiesPress.com | info@libertiespress.com
+353 (1) 415 1224

Trade enquiries to CMD BookSource
Tel: +353 (1) 294 2560
Fax: +353 (1) 294 2564

Distributed in the United States by
Dufour Editions
PO Box 7 | Chester Springs | Pennsylvania | 19425

and in Australia by
James Bennett Pty Limited | InBooks
3 Narabang Way | Belrose NSW 2085

Copyright © Éamonn Ó Catháin, 2009

The author has asserted his moral rights.

ISBN: 978–1–905483–89–1

2 4 6 8 10 9 7 5 3 1
A CIP record for this title is available from the British Library

Cover design by Sin É Design
Internal design by Liberties Press
Printed in Ireland by Colour Books

THE HARD TIMES COOKBOOK

ÉAMONN Ó CATHÁIN

CONTENTS

INTRODUCTION

Nothing ever impressed me as much as French home cooking – though if I'd arrived in Italy instead, I'd probably be saying much the same about Italian cooking. But France it was, and while in the thirty-odd years since I first arrived there, France has changed significantly, and its gastronomic treasures are more often hidden than evident, it still had a profound influence on my culinary thinking. That tradition of self-suffiency, of barter, of seasons, of the *potager*, persists. This tradition has allowed France and its Continental Latin neighbours to weather the financial crisis much better than we, the Irish.

I was lucky to discover rural domestic French cooking at a relatively young age by spending a lot of time in the garden, kitchen and dining room of the mother of the girl that I was walking out with at the time. Apart from the pleasure of the delicious food that I was fattened up on twice a day, I was mesmerised by the organisation, the thrift and the execution of this *bonne chère*, which rarely seemed to repeat itself. You'll have no difficulty in believing that I was there at mealtimes, a lot. A rare instance of a guy going out with a girl for her mother!

The woman of the house bought bread from the nearest good *boulangerie* and staples like rice, butter, oil and vinegar from the local grocer's, but most of the food came from the garden – from the ingredients for soup to the herbs used in the home-made *gniaule* or *digestif*, not to mention the vividly yellow eggs from the squawking chickens, and the roast rabbit (in mustard sauce) we had every so often. Of course, she would also buy meat locally in the cleanest and freshest-smelling butcher's I have ever known, and fish from the van that drove through the area and stopped at every house twice a week. To this day, I remember the enormous mackerel we all fed from, set regally in the centre of the table, baked in local Muscadet, with onions and tomatoes and garlic – the hugest mackerel you ever did see!

I also worked hard for a while in the fields of the hinterland of St Mâlo, fed three times a day by the farmer's wife, who was thrilled that this *irlandais* was so appreciative of her food, and who imparted some of her recipes and techniques to me. I loved the *pâté de campagne* and beer that we got at 9.30 every morning, after exactly ninety minutes of work, but how I longed for the whistle of the 12.09 express as it sped towards St Mâlo, signalling to me that our three-course lunch (based in part on the fruit of my labours: the *carottes, patates* and *choux*) was just twenty-one minutes away.

Later on, I would visit the north of Italy and find similar methods and a similar love of food, and even later in my life I would discover joyful Spain and its omnipresent bite-sized cuisine. But I never forgot those first lessons in rural Brittany, which taught me *how to eat* and inspired me to learn to cook for myself, to re-create those sublime meals.

Many of the methods I saw and the dishes I ate formed the basis of the cooking I would practise in my own restaurant a few years later; the food was initially the food of the French home and the local café, the streetside restaurant and the *routier* – the quality of the latter judged by the number of heavy-duty lorries parked outside at lunchtime. While I eventually embraced 'smart' food and got caught up in the intense competition between restaurants that marked Ireland's food scene in the eighties, I never really deserted the classic dishes of France.

I opened that restaurant, I now know, in a

recession. Opening the restaurant wasn't so much a brave move on my part as a foolhardy one: I had no plan to speak of. Luckily, I got away with it, mainly because I hit the right price point and served food that I loved. The Ireland of the early eighties wasn't really ready for that sort of food then – it triumphs these days – and if I had a cent for every time I've heard 'You'd make a fortune these days', I'd be blah blah blah.

But I do still do it: at home, just not for a paying audience. Things inevitably come full circle, and here we are, once again, in the middle – or maybe it's not even the beginning – of a singularly tough recession. In the eighties, I remember how traditional cooking was frowned upon; trendy terms such as 'rustic' and 'classic' had not yet been hijacked for restaurant use. I remember, too, reading how the yuppies of the late eighties didn't want breadcrumbs in their *gaspacho* to thicken it, nor fourteen layers of the same breadcrumbs on their cassoulet or béchamel sauce with anything, thank you very much.

Puh-leeze, we no longer work in fields, they would whine. Yuppies, bless them, are no longer with us. Banks are on their last legs, some governments appear to be incompetent, financial markets are in turmoil, and the property market is in freefall. But the fields are still there, and we still have to eat in order to stay alive. And the consumer is benefiting. Our largest supermarkets are piled high with two- and three-for-one deals: cheap pasta, butter, bread, vegetables and mince.

Then there is their latest innovation, the 'meal-for-two deal', including a bottle of wine. It seems great on the face of it, but is it? At the time of writing, a story is doing the rounds that the fat content of some of their salads is higher than that of a typical McDonald's meal. If this is true, it is bad news for your waistline, and illustrates the urgent need for us to take control once more of what we put in our bodies, for the sake of both our waistline and our wallet. The bottom line is the fact that these two-for-one meals all taste exactly the same and should be regarded with a jaundiced eye.

Hence this book: it's time for thrift, for real cooking, and for a rethink of our relationship with the supermarket. Breadcrumbs are back! So too is shopping at the local butcher, the vegetable shop and the weekly market. (As idyllic as the picture of having your own *potager* may be, we can't all do this, or even be a farmer's wife.) Awareness of seasons is crucial when it comes to getting the best value and, above all, the best flavour. We need to look at the fridge and see it brimming with possibilities, not half-empty. We need to buy wisely and with parsimony, and above all to revive and revisit older, forgotten recipes. A book that has long influenced me is *Cuisine du Terroir*: a number of leading French chefs collected recipes which were in danger of being lost forever. Recent trips to France revealed a proliferation of restaurants doing granny-style food, with older favourites like beef cheeks, brandades and various blanquettes gracing even the trendiest tables once more.

This book will also present those recipes that avoid the overcomplicated and embrace the tasty, the cheap and, above all, the cheerful. These are convivial recipes, ones with which to break bread together, ones that will go far, ones that will put a smile on your face, and ones that will not cost the earth. It is important in these hard times to continue to eat well, where 'well' means both healthily and sumptuously.

To get us started, I'm going to list those ingredients which I recommend you always have in your kitchen, plus a selection of kitchen equipment that you should have to hand – and a few tips as to which implements you can do without.

And the recipes? These will all be my own, gathered from my experiences and travels: the things that I really enjoy eating, dishes that I have shared with friends or are ideal for eating alone, dishes based on ingredients that can be found locally, and easily. Unless otherwise stated, the recipes are designed to feed four people. I hope you like them.

THE ESSENTIALS:
INGREDIENTS

In my kitchen, there are various basic ingredients I would never be without. Some are obvious but will be repeated here nonetheless; others are less so. You don't have to follow this to the letter, but if you have most of them, you will always have the basis of a satisfying meal, especially if plans change and visitors become unexpected lunch or dinner guests.

Salt
Pepper
Sea salt
Groundnut oil (aka peanut oil)
Olive oil
Butter
White-wine vinegar
Plain flour

Buckwheat flour
Yeast
A hard cheese, such as Gruyère or Emmental
A soft cheese such as Camembert
White and red wine
Spaghetti or spaghettini
Tagliatelle
Short macaroni
Eggs
Ham
Dijon mustard
*A little jar of dried herbs, such as herbes de
    Provence*
Tinned tomatoes
Tinned chickpeas
Tinned petits pois
Couscous
Rice
Polenta
Low-fat yoghurt or fromage frais
Lemons

Utensils

Here is a non-exhaustive list of utensils and equipment you need in order to cook well. Some of the items, such as the all-purpose pot (hereinafter referred to as the 'very large pot'), serve double functions. That pot can also be a stock pot; a saucepan can be used to make tea in; a coffee grinder will of course grind coffee but, after a wipe-down, can also quickly chop herbs (just remember to wipe it down again before grinding coffee in it); the base of a tagine will serve as a casserole dish, a *paellera*, or even just a big pan. I get great use out of mine.

1 large all-purpose pot
1 small saucepan
1 larger saucepan
1 wire-mesh sieve
A food processor
A medium non-stick frying pan
1 wooden spoon
1 metal spoon
1 slotted spoon
1 balloon whisk
1 colander
1 coffee grinder
1 roasting tray (battered, perhaps, but clean)
A tagine

A casserole dish
A ridged grill pan
A pestle and mortar
A salad drier
A steamer (the Thai bamboo steamers available in
*   most Asian supermarkets are just the job)*

Some Basic Recipes You Shouldn't Be Without

Scattered throughout this book are recipes for the sauces, stocks and accompaniments that hold the dishes together, but here in one short chapter are some of those basic techniques that transform a simple, everyday dish into something special.

Vinaigrette I

In general, a vinaigrette is composed of three parts oil to one part vinegar, with a little salt and pepper. To my surprise, there are people who still do not know how to make one, or who will waste money on a bottled one from a supermarket. These products are not only nothing like the real thing but, thanks to the unnecessary addition of sugar, are also unhealthy. The simplest recipe for vinaigrette is:

1 tablespoon white-wine vinegar
3 tablespoons groundnut oil
A pinch of salt and a grinding of black pepper

You may substitute other oils and vinegars, but I like to use the virtually flavourless groundnut oil to show off a flavoured vinegar. If the dressing is going on a simple green salad, it is a good idea to salt the leaves and then apply the unsalted dressing. This spreads the salt better. In France, they say you should toss a salad thirty-six times. The Italians just put the oil and vinegar on the table and let people add it to the salad themselves.

Vinaigrette II

In this variation on the classic dressing, you begin by whisking together oil and a tablespoon of mustard before adding the vinegar to form a thickish, mustard-based sauce vinaigrette.

1 tablespoon white-wine vinegar
3 tablespoons groundnut oil
1 generous teaspoon Dijon mustard
Salt and pepper

Vinaigrette III (sauce moutarde)

This version is much heavier on the mustard and is made like a mayonnaise but without the egg. You simply whisk together the mustard with the oil (adding the oil slowly), then a little vinegar, plus seasoning. It can form the basis of many other dressings.

Two tablespoons Dijon mustard
Oil to thicken (olive or groundnut)
1 tablespoon white-wine vinegar

This sauce can happily accommodate chopped parsley, chopped gherkins, chopped hard-boiled egg, chopped shallots or chopped garlic for an even more entertaining experience. Use less mustard if you don't like it too strong.

Mayonnaise

Mayonnaise is closely related to the sauce above; this time, egg yolk is used in the emulsion. There is nothing quite like real home-made mayonnaise, using quality ingredients. It should have a good, pungent flavour of mustard, and a light-yellow colour. The jars of mayonnaise available in the supermarkets in no way resemble the real thing.

> *150ml oil (groundnut if you want the flavour of the mustard to stand out; otherwise, use olive)*
> *1 tablespoon white-wine vinegar*
> *1 egg yolk*
> *Pinch of salt*
> *1 dollop Dijon mustard*

Begin by mixing the egg yolk and mustard together in a wide bowl which you have placed on a dishcloth or sheet of kitchen roll. (The cloth or paper will hold the bowl in place while you whisk.) No whisk? A fork will do nicely, with some inspired legerdemain from your good self.

Then add the oil – very slowly at first and, as it is incorporated, more quickly. The mayonnaise will become thicker as you whisk. When all the oil has been absorbed and the mayonnaise is so thick that a teaspoon will stand up in it, add vinegar to achieve the desired consistency.

That's it: season to taste, and it's ready to consume. No, it isn't straightforward, and yes, it may take a little practice to get right. Here's a tip: if it turns on you, rescue it by throwing a little chilled water into it.

Pesto

For a while, pesto was everywhere, being used for all manner of purposes for which it was never intended. For that reason, I went off it, but now that it (along with tomato-and-fennel bread) is no longer flavour of the decade, I've started to enjoy it again. Here's how you make your own. (In this instance, I'm not decrying the bought stuff, which is generally good. Trouble is, it's expensive – and not half as good as what you can make yourself.)

A large handful of basil leaves
Some freshly grated Parmesan
1 clove of garlic
About 130ml olive oil
30g pine nuts

You can do this the long way, with a pestle and mortar and and lots of elbow grease, or using a food processor and a little judgement. The garlic, basil and pine kernels go into that processor, but a nice little extra trick is to toast them first. Pine nuts burn easily, so you need to be careful. Toast them on your non-stick pan, and keep moving them around. When they've taken on a bit of colour, put them in the food processor. Blend, but use the pulse button, so that you get a chunky consistency and don't overprocess them. Add the oil, until the correct consistency has been achieved. Pour into a receptacle, and if salt is needed, add a little.

*

With these four sauces in your fridge, you are, as they repeatedly say, laughing. And with the exception of mayonnaise (which should be eaten within two days), they can all be made in quantity.

*

Bouquet garni

Every so often, I'll be calling for a bouquet garni in these recipes. It's simply the following aromatic herbs, tied with a piece of string

1 sprig of thyme
1 bay leaf
A few sprigs of parsley

SOUPS

A young French friend of mine – a chef – once remarked to me that he didn't like soups; a curious thing to say, given that his nation has given the world so many fine soups, and has even given the English language the words 'soup' and 'supper' (from the French verb *souper*). Since then, I've discovered a whole substrata of French people – probably from those areas where the Franks were more populous than the Gauls – who don't like hot drinks (hot chocolate, coffee, tea or soups) at all at all. Weirdos.

Even more curious, I've lately come round to his way of thinking, finding many soups heavy, too filling and, in some rare cases, dull and boring. This, I concede, is an odd opening to a chapter on soups, but do please bear with me. For, despite approaching senility, I continue to like those soups which are essentially based on one main ingredient, where something terrific is created from something quite humble, which are quick and easy to make, toothsome and invigorating, and surefooted in terms of taste and flavour.

These are the ones we are looking for: soups that are cheap to produce but anything but cheap-tasting. They should be made in bulk and can then feed a family throughout the week, or be frozen for use at a later date. Some can be made quickly for a simple supper for one or two; these soups not only provide the goodness a body needs but also provide almost instant gratification, without the need to reach for the nearest overpriced tin on the supermarket shelf.

Here, then, is a short collection of the soups I never tire of: like all the recipes in this book, they have been tried and tested. They come from all over: there are classics from France but also some happy blow-ins from places whose food I have discovered more recently and which excite and inspire me. Many require the minimum of ingredients, relying instead on centuries of thrift, know-how and tradition to produce something that will satisfy. Many require a stock, so let's start there. I noticed that a lot of the supermarkets have a wide range of stocks on display these days in dried, gellified or liquid form; I notice, too, that many of them are fairly expensive. Make your own, I say. Make this one.

Chicken stock:

1 stick of celery, roughly chopped

1 onion, studded with a couple of cloves

2 leeks; discard the dark green leaves, and cut the white part into rounds

180g carrots, sliced thickly

A bouquet garni (a small sprig of thyme, a small bunch of parsley and a bay leaf, all wrapped and tied in one of those leaves from the leek that I told you to discard)

1 chicken carcass, or just the wings. These are to be blanched and then refreshed (run under cold water). If you can get a boiling fowl, so much the better, because I will be giving a recipe for the classic poule au pot.

Place the chicken carcass in a large pot and cover with water (around two and a half litres). Bring this to the boil and immediately lower the heat and allow to simmer. Using a metal spoon, skim any impurities that rise the surface and then add all the vegetables. (You can substitute the ones I listed for, say, carrot peelings, outer onion leaves, or bits of other aromatic vegetables from the previous day's cooking.) Leave to cook gently for ninety minutes to two hours. Note: no garlic, no salt.

Strain the stock through a sieve, leave it to cool and use when needed. It can also be frozen for later use. Hurrah!

Lettuce and carrot soup

Let's get started on our soups: here's a real beauty. I baulked at it many years ago because of the notion of lettuce in a soup but, despite what you might think, the lettuce remains crunchy in the hot soup and is an excellent foil to the main ingredient, the carrot. It's deliciously simple, and has the added bonus of using up those Little Gems which looked so nice in the shop but you then forgot about and left sitting in the bottom of the fridge.

500ml plain water or chicken stock (see page 29)
1 lettuce (romaine or cos lettuce is ideal, as is Little
    Gem. Should you have some that are a little,
    shall we say, tired, remove the outer leaves and
    discard, using only the hearts.)
2 shallots
1 onion, chopped finely
1 bunch of parsley
A little butter
Salt and black pepper
Half a dozen carrots, peeled and diced

Finely chop the shallots and sweat them in a little butter. Add the onion and allow it all to cook for a few more minutes before adding the carrots.

After a few minutes, add the water or stock, bring to the boil, reduce the heat and allow to simmer for twenty minutes.

After this time, transfer to a food processor, together with the chopped parsley, and blend until smooth. Add the salt and pepper to taste. (This trusty approach is never more important than when making soups, for while it may be possible to remove the effects over over-salting (add rice or potatoes to absorb the excess salt), nothing can be done about over-peppering.

Shred the lettuce very finely, place a little in the bottom of the soup bowls and pour the soup on top. The lettuce will float to the top and will look appetising against the pale orange of the carrots. Serve piping hot.

A simple leek and potato soup

There seem to be few dissenters when it comes to leek and potato soup. It's just one of those that hits the spot and pleases most people, whether in its original rich form of vichyssoise or, as here, in a more pared-down form. We don't have any money to be spending on cream, so let's keep that in reserve for a recipe that will need it. (Though should you have some lying around in the fridge – or indeed even a little crème fraiche – then by all means use it.)

> *1 chopped onion*
> *3 medium leeks, trimmed, washed and chopped*
> *4 largish potatoes, chopped*
> *Butter*
> *Cream or crème fraiche (optional)*
> *Chervil (optional)*
> *Water or chicken stock (see page 29)*

Begin by melting about 25g of the butter in that very large pot you bought, and soften the chopped onion in it. At the same time, heat the stock or water separately (in a different pot, which you may or may not own; when I get stuck and find myself potless, I use the breadbin, having first removed all the bread).

Leave the onion for about ten minutes and then, when it's golden, add the leeks. Leave these to soften for about five minutes, then add the potatoes.

When this is done, add enough of the water or stock to cover all the vegetables, and season with a little salt.

Bring to the boil and then leave to simmer for around twenty minutes, or until the potatoes are cooked.

Blend the soup in a food processor or using some other blending implement.

You could serve this with a little cream or crème fraiche, or garnish it with a little chervil, should you be able to find some. A pinch of nutmeg will also enhance this classic soup. One more thing: our first two soups have the potential for being vegetarian-friendly, so the advice to use water instead of chicken stock is sound. Just follow the sweating instructions, season well but judiciously, and all will be fine.

French onion soup

The all-time classic! Never fails to please, great for using up stale baguette and cheese that has hardened round the edges, sorts good chefs from the also-rans – but also, like a lot of French recipes, is not exactly vegetarian-friendly, by virtue of the meat stock used in it. Hard cheese, as my da used to say.

Beef stock:

French onion soup is one of the simplest soups you can make, but its simplicity is cunning. It relies on a decent beef stock (its base or *fond*); without this, it will not be remotely successful. You can make a passable effort using one of those new sachets of liquid stock (or the gellifed stuff). But if you make this beef stock in your own good time, you will have it ready for French onion soup, when the mood takes you, or for some other recipes in this book. Believe me, it is fun, and worth the effort.

3kg beef bones (get these from your butcher and ask him to crack or chop them)
3 or 4 carrots
3 sticks of celery

3 leeks
1 head of garlic
2 onions
A little thyme and a bay leaf
A little tomato puree

Unlike the chicken stock, you need to roast the bones for this one, so preheat your oven to around 200 degrees and give them a good roasting for around half an hour. You will need some class of a roasting tray. When this is done, remove from oven, drain off the fat and transfer the bones to your wonderful very large pot – which, by now, you're really glad you bought. Cover the bones in plenty of cold water (around four litres, if the pot can hold it) and bring to the boil.

Prepare your vegetables during this time: peel and chop the carrots, quarter the onions, roughly chop the leeks, cut the garlic in two, and chop up the celery. Fry these ingredients one by one (yes, even the carrots), leave to rest on kitchen roll and then combine them all for one last merry dance on the pan, together with the bay leaf, thyme and tomato puree, over a low heat for about ten minutes. Use a small amount of a neutral oil to do this, vegetable or groundnut (though the latter is a bit dearer). When the frying is done, drain off any excess oil and turn your attentions once more to the boiling-having-been-roasted beef bones.

First, you need to skim off any scum that has risen to the top of the water, using your shiny metal spoon. When this is done, you need to add all the fried vegetables and leave to simmer over a low heat for quite a while. 'Quite a while' means hours. About five or six hours, to be vaguely precise. Skim frequently during this time, removing any impurities or fat that may appear.

Finally, strain this stock as best you can, preferably through a muslin cloth into another container, perhaps a second all-purpose pot, or maybe a large metal bowl big enough to hold all the strained liquid. You then need to reduce that liquid further and, when it's cooled, store it in the fridge in a sealed container. When cool, any remaining fat will solidify and can be removed.

Yes, I hear you say, you could just go and buy a puny, non-manly stock, but you won't have as much fun, you won't be able to go off and read a book, and you certainly won't make a French onion soup as excellent as this one.

The soup bit:

Onions! 6 of them (the best you can find)
A little groundnut oil
45g butter (Use unsalted. Too expensive? Use ordinary butter, but be mindful elsewhere when tempted to add salt.)

6 cloves of garlic
1 litre of the delicious beef stock that you have spent
    six hours making (or an exciting sachet of same
    from your local emporium instead)
A handful of fresh thyme
Half a bottle of hearty, cheapish red wine – prefer-
    ably French, definitely delicious
Salt and black pepper
A small sprig of parsley
1 baguette of bread, preferably stale
100g Gruyère or Emmenthal cheese

OK. You need to slice all those onions. Peel them, throw away any dark green outer leaf, cut them in half, and then slice them into uniform crescents. Get your large pot (now freed up after the six-hour marathon stock-making session), add the oil and butter to that, and allow to foam. Throw in the onions with the thyme and cook over a very low heat until the onions are transparent. Never let them colour. The colour of this soup comes from the wine and the stock used, not from browning the onions. When they are transparent and soft, chop all the garlic up finely and add to the onions, leaving to cook slowly for another twenty minutes.

Now add the wine and boil vigorously until most of it has evaporated. Add your litre of most excellent beef stock and cook for a further fifty minutes. At this time, check the seasoning and add more, if necessary.

The soup is ready, and all that remains is to make the croutons of bread, with their cheesy topping. Slice the bread. If it is stale, mix with a little oil to revive it. Then put into the oven at 200 degrees and allow to crispen. Turn them over and cover with plenty of grated Gruyère or Emmenthal. Note that you cannot use cheddar, Gouda, Jarlsberger or anything else (though it doesn't matter if the Gruyère or Emmenthal is a bit hard or tough; in fact, that would be perfect). Bake or grill on that side until golden.

Ladle the soup into individual bowls, put the croutons on top, and sprinkle with parsley if desired.

Garlic soup (tourin à l'ail)

Now we're hitting our stride. I once had a book of old French recipes that were in danger of being lost forever, and discovered, made and loved *tourin à l'ail*, or garlic soup. I've been making it ever since (despite the fact that someone half-inched the book); it really is a clever way of making something out of almost nothing. It costs very little, which makes up for the teensy bit more expensive onion soup above, which needed wine. Since then, I've discovered some more garlic soup recipes. I'll let you have those too – but nothing will ever displace the original in my affections.

> *6 heads of garlic*
> *1 onion*
> *1 baguette, or loaf of country bread*
> *Goose fat (optional)*
> *3 tablespoons olive oil*
> *2 tablespoons white-wine vinegar*
> *2 litres water (or chicken stock)*
> *1 egg per person*
> *Salt and black pepper*

First peel the garlic, slice in half, and remove the green 'germ' from each one. Chop all the garlic very finely and then gently fry in a little olive oil, without letting it brown. (If you have goose or duck fat left over from Christmas, you could use that for a true taste of Perigord, from where this soup comes.) Add the finely chopped onion and allow to cook with the garlic. When golden, add the water and bring to the boil, then reduce the heat and leave to simmer. It only takes about twenty-five minutes, after which time you may leave it as it is or quickly whizz it up in a processor for a smoother soup (not traditional). Season.

Break the eggs, then separate the whites from the yolks. Slice the bread and rub with olive oil. Whisk the yolks until smooth, and add the vinegar. Everything is just about ready for the magic to happen.

When ready to serve, fry the croutons on a pan until golden. Place these in the bottom of a bowl. Whisk the egg whites quickly into the hot soup, where they will cook and go stringy. Pour a little of the egg-and-vinegar mix into the bottom of each serving bowl and pour the soup on top, stirring as you go. The soup will immediately change in look and texture, and thicken. It will also smell wonderful, your nostrils being wooed by the divine whiff of cooked garlic and vinegar. Place a crouton on top and sprinkle . . . well, with nothing at all, actually. It's pretty darn perfect.

Some tips. This delightful soup (great for cleaning out the system and great for your blood) requires little more than the ingredients mentioned. (For vegetarians, use water instead of the chicken stock.) If you want a thicker soup, add a little flour to the garlic-and-onion mixture, allowing it to cook for a minute or two just before you add the water or stock. Leave out the egg whites if that doesn't appeal to you, but do try and use them elsewhere. Don't bother with the food processor if you don't have one – it doesn't really need it, if the garlic is cut up finely enough. Do not use malt vinegar.

I can't tell you just how delicious this soup is.

A garlic soup from Spain

Here's a garlic soup from Spain, a country which I discovered recently at the tender age of fifty-plus. Allegedly it's the original gaspacho, made from garlic and served cold on hot days. I hear there'll be one of those next year in Ireland.

Sherry vinegar is wonderful but expensive; fortunately it goes a long way, and we'll be using it elsewhere in this very tome. As for the rest of the ingredients, they're cheap enough, especially the breadcrumbs and the water. For added sexiness, you could put some grapes in it, though it's delicious without.

180g bread, preferably stale
250g raw skinned almonds
3 cloves of garlic
1 litre of ice-cold water
500g grapes (Muscatel), seeded and cut in half (optional)
1 tablespoon sherry vinegar
Olive oil
Pinch of salt

Rub or chop the bread into breadcrumbs – a nice touch is to toast them (sauté them on a dry non-stick pan to achieve this) before proceeding with the recipe.

Place the breadcrumbs, garlic, almonds and salt together in a blender and pulse it all until a paste begins to form, adding the olive oil a little at a time. Then add the vinegar and transfer to a bowl.

Add the water and the grapes, if you're using them, and some crushed ice if desired.

Leave it in the bowl in the fridge for about thirty minutes before serving.

Garlic soup with lardons

This is a heftier soup, and a little more involved than the *tourin à l'ail*. It's for winter days and for those who want meat in their soup but no eggs.

4 heads of garlic
1 onion
2 shallots
1 kg potatoes
1 small bunch of fresh thyme
2 litres chicken stock
4 rashers of bacon
Salt and black pepper
A little olive oil
Some stale bread, cut into croutons and fried in the pan or roasted in oil in the oven

Peel and chop all the garlic, followed by the onion, then the shallots.

Sweat the garlic in a little olive oil for one or two minutes, then add the chopped onion and the shallots. Cook until soft and translucent but do not allow to colour.

Peel and roughly chop the potatoes and add them to the garlic and onions. Cover with the chicken stock.

Mix well, then allow to simmer gently for around thirty minutes, or until the potatoes are cooked. Blend in a mixer. Taste and adjust the seasoning with salt and freshly ground black pepper.

Pan-fry the bacon until crispy, then chop into small dice. Lightly toast the croutons.

When ready to serve, place equal amounts of bacon and croutons in each bowl, then gently pour the soup on top.

Fish soup

We can't have a chapter on soups that doesn't have a recipe for fish soup in it; sometimes I get so desirous for fish soup, I shake, I tremble, I fall down, I pick myself up and I run to the kitchen and make it. Surely, you ask, fish soup is an awesome task, requiring Mediterranean fish of all shapes and colours, imported at great price, and involving much toil, a *fumet de poisson* and an apartment in Marseilles? Well, no, it doesn't have to be bouillabaisse, it doesn't even have to have much (or indeed any) fish in it . . . it just has to have the taste of fish and the taste of Marseilles – plus a coterie of things to put in it, like cheese and croutons, if not *rouille*, the unctuous garlic-based emulsion indispensable for fish soup and served on the side and added at the last minute. Have a pastis, then make this.

> *Fish trimmings (leftovers from another recipe, or ask the fishmonger for them; a kilo would be an elegant sufficiency; heads, tails, spines – all good)*
> *2 leeks*
> *3 onions*
> *2 carrots*
> *1 stick of celery*

1 glass of white wine (optional)
1 bouquet garni
1 tablespoon sea salt
1 teaspoon peppercorns
Salt and pepper

Wash and peel the vegetables, and chop them up. Put them all in your very large pot with the fish trimmings and cover the lot with cold water. Add the sea salt plus the white wine, the peppercorns and the celery stick, and bring it to the boil. Cover it and allow to simmer for at least half an hour. That's it! All you have to do now is strain it through a *chinois*, if you have one, or through a wire-mesh colander or sieve if you don't. If you have some old bread around, make garlic croutons with them by cutting them into small squares, rubbing with garlic and a little olive oil, and placing in the oven for a few minutes. If you have some Gruyère cheese lying around, grate it, serve on the side in a little ramekin and then add it to the soup at the table. For a more consistent soup, you could add some of those tiny pasta shapes, such as orzo or ziti or diti, or whatever it is they're called. You'll find them in any good Italian food shop. If you do this, add the pasta to the sieved soup and allow to cook for at least another five minutes before serving.

Harira

This Moroccan soup is one of the world's greatest soups; it's eaten there to break the fast during the holy month of Ramadan. It isn't complicated to make and gives a fabulous result when the recipe is followed exactly. I should know: for years I thought I was making it properly but have since realised (or rather, been made to realise) that I wasn't.

This is the right way.

A little Moroccan olive oil (try and seek out 'El Ouazzania' – it's worth it)
2 onions
2 cloves of garlic
1 teaspoon cumin
2 teaspoons paprika
Pinch of cinnamon
Pinch of saffron
1 tin chickpeas
2 tins chopped tomatoes
Small bunch of parsley
Small bunch of celery leaves
Bunch of coriander
1 stick of celery
1 litre beef stock

1 bay leaf
2 tablespoons tomato puree
500g lamb, cut from the shoulder (ideally should be
    halal – and must be if you have Muslim guests)
1 lemon

First, trim the lamb. All excess fat should be removed, and the meat should be cut into very small chunks.

Crush the garlic and chop the onion. Heat the oil (about two tablespoons-full) in – guess what? – your big pot, of course, and add the garlic and onion to it, allowing to soften (but not brown) over a low heat. After a couple of minutes, add the chopped celery. After six or seven minutes, add the meat to this and allow to colour, turning up the heat a little.

Now add the ground cumin, paprika, cinnamon, saffron and bay leaf to this, and allow to cook until they release their odours. Follow this with the tomato puree and allow to cook for a further three minutes. Finally, add your beef stock (told you it would come in handy) and bring it all to the boil.

Chop the coriander (keep a little back for garnish), parsley and celery leaves and add these to the soup, together with the drained chickpeas and tomatoes. Return to the boil, then reduce the heat and simmer until the meat is tender. Taste to check this, but if the lamb is cut up small, this should take forty-five minutes to one hour. Correct the seasoning.

Serve with bread, chopped coriander, a little olive oil on the side and a quarter of lemon, which each person can then squeeze into the soup.

White haricot bean soup

If I was rather keen on my Perigord garlic soup earlier in this chapter, then I'm just about as keen on this delicious recipe for white haricot bean soup. It's one of those indefinable stood-the-test-of-time peasant concotions that relies on little more then haricot beans and water, yet its texture and taste are remarkable. There are of course many variants and many ways of enhancing the soup's satisfaction-per-mouthful factor – such as a garlic underbelly or a drizzle of olive oil – and we'll note those after this, the elementary recipe. Soups based on haricot beans can be found in areas such as Tuscany and parts of France where, of course, it reaches its apogee as 'Garbure', but for today, let's keep it simple and cheerful. (For a more elaborate bean dish, we'll be looking at the wonderful cassoulet later (page 121).)

350g of dry white beans (haricot or cannellini)
1 bouquet garni
A little olive oil
1 onion, chopped
1 carrot, chopped
1 stick of celery, chopped
3 tomatoes, peeled and chopped

2 cloves of garlic, crushed
Pinch of turmeric
Salt and pepper

Best to leave the beans to soak in plenty of cold water the previous night.

Take your big pot and boil the beans in it in fresh cold water for almost two hours, or until soft and tender. During this time, sauté your chopped onion, celery and carrot in the olive oil for a few minutes, then add the garlic and the tomatoes. Add the turmeric (which is getting great press these days as a superfood and allegedly an antidote to Alzheimer's) and the bouquet garni, and remove just before the end of cooking. Transfer to a food processor and blend until smooth, topping up with a little extra water if needed.

Variants and extra ingredients:

This soup lends itself very well to a glass of white wine added during the cooking, some parsley or chervil, a drizzle of olive oil, a drizzle of olive oil which has had loads of finely chopped parsley added to it (to give a nice green contrast to the off-white colour of the soup), savoy cabbage, shallots and . . . chorizo. Not only is some chorizo (cut into strips and fried for a few seconds) really tasty on top of each bowl of bean soup, but it is also a lovely way of using up those old slices of chorizo you never got round to eating and which are, well, a bit hard around the edges. Fear not, the frying will revive them, just don't cook them for too long (about five seconds in a hot pan should do it).

STARTERS

Ever since I was little, I have loved tomatoes. My mother tells tales on me of how, having bought a pound of them, I would be left sitting in my Tansad (a pram of the 1950s, folks) and have them consumed through the brown paper bag (after biting a hole in it) before we even got home, while she was busy shopping for other things. Since then, I have enjoyed the tomato in all its forms – as a sauce, a garnish, in salads, stuffed (Oh, there's an idea! We'll come back to that), in tarts and terrines, chopped, sliced and seeded. First up, here's a simple recipe from France which first taught me how to enjoy the flavour of the tomato on its own, followed by the same thing Spanish-style.

Tomato salad I

At least two plump tomatoes per person (Preferably Spanish, definitely not Dutch. And before any howls of protest ensue, let me tell you that even the Dutch call these insults to tomatoes 'water bombs'. Best place to find decent fruit and vegetables if you don't have access to a market? Lidl. A German supermarket for a discerning German clientele first and foremost. Stocks good Spanish tomatoes.)

Olive oil
White-wine or cider or spirit vinegar
Salt and pepper

All you have to do is slice the tomatoes thinly. (Discard the top slice, where the stalk is.) Then arrange them attractively on a plate, allowing each slice to overlap. Make a vinaigrette with three parts olive oil to one part vinegar, season with the black pepper only, then sprinkle the tomatoes with a little salt before spooning the sauce over the tomatoes. Simple enough, very, very red, and quite delicious. What makes it special are two things, as imparted to me way back when. First, use olive oil instead of groundnut oil, and secondly, no mustard in the vinaigrette sauce. Too simple? Variants include thinly sliced hard-boiled egg (arranged in between the tomato slices), finely chopped shallots scattered gaily over the lot, and maybe a little parsley. But the original basic recipe has stood me in fine stead over the years and remained my way of thinking on all things tomato salad-related until . . .

Tomato salad II

Two years ago, I went for the first time ever to Spain, a country I had deliberately avoided for many years, confusing its heat and dust with that of Mexico, I think (mainly due to *The Adventures of Zorro the Fox*, read while I was a heat- and dust-phobic young fella). So finally, as a fifty-something, I got to enjoy the multi-layered pleasures of Spain's tapas scene, glasses of fino, its reassuring-for-an-Irishman potatoes-with-everything culture (in the south, anyway) and, well, more tomatoes. This salad was served to me in a fish restaurant as a curtain-raiser without ceremony or enquiry. It just arrived on the table as a 'Why wouldn't you want this?' prelude to the meal. What struck me, apart from its excellence, was that the recipe had no doubt been the same for decades, and was probably pertinent to the establishment in question. Here's how I put it back together again.

Two tomatoes per person (same rules of origin apply as for the tomato salad above)
Olive oil
Sherry vinegar
Garlic (lots of it)
Parsley

Sea salt (The Spanish love Maldon, so if your budget can accommodate it, get that for a true authentic British taste of Spain. Ever tried their smoked variant? It's fab.)

Once again, slice the tomatoes thinly and arrange them attractively on a plate, going heavy on the overlapping. This time, crush the peeled garlic cloves with the back of a knife and chop them roughly. (It isn't much of an exaggeration to say that a whole head of garlic could go on top of the tomatoes in this manner, but adjust for your palate.) Scatter the garlic all over the tomatoes, and follow with a light sprinkling of the sea salt.

I find that doing this before saucing 'works' the tomatoes a little, drawing more flavour from them, particularly if you have tomatoes that are somewhat less tasty than those of Spain.

When ready to serve, spoon over two or three generous tablespoonfuls of the sherry vinegar (granted, this is expensive, but one bottle will go a long way, and I will use it for other recipes later on), followed by twice as much olive oil. Finally, a few pinches of parsley. (What struck me when eating this was the marvellous relief afforded by the odd hint of parsley and the odd flake of sea salt.) Note, no black pepper. Strictly not needed.

Have lots of bread to hand, to mop up the sauce.

Warm potato and sausage salad

This is a delicious salad that can be eaten all year round and has never failed to impress anyone I've served it to, no matter how sophisticated their palate. Simple and rustic, it could very feasibly be put together from leftovers. It makes a delicious first course but could certainly be served as a main course instead.

> *2 or 3 potatoes per person (Preferably waxy potatoes for a salad of distinction; charlottes will do. The 'balls of flour' so beloved by the Irish – though, I confess, disliked by me since infancy – will not work as they will only spoil the presentation and overall texture. The potatoes can be cooked specifically for this salad or those left over from the previous night's meal could be used. In any case, peel them.)*
>
> *2 shallots*
> *Small bunch of parsley*
> *Groundnut oil*
> *Dijon mustard*
> *Salt and black pepper*
> *White-wine, cider or spirit vinegar*
> *Sausages (Preferably Toulouse or an Italian coarse sausage. If these are not available, seek out the*

*best coarse pure pork sausage you can find and
can afford. Sorry, pale, anaemic, chemical-ridden
travesties of sausages will simply not do.)*

First, peel the potatoes and then cook them 'just
so'. (If using leftovers, we'll come to them in a
minute.) Save on electricity, washing up, extra
utensils and so on by plunging the sausage of your
choice into the same water for about five minutes
to cook them through. Remove and brown under
the grill. When the potatoes are cooked, remove,
refresh and slice, but keep the water in the pot.
Tasty, tasty, very, very tasty.

Now for the vinaigrette sauce. You will need a lot,
so use at least nine tablespoons of oil and place
this in a large mixing bowl. Add a generous dollop
of French Dijon mustard. (I stress French, even
though it might seem obvious: Dijon mustard
made by other nationalities is just not the same,
as they simply haven't grasped that you shouldn't
put sugar in it.) Whisk this in (using a fork if you
don't have a whisk) until it's fully incorporated,
then add three tablespoons of vinegar to dilute
and lengthen and, you know, make vinaigrette. (Incidentally, if you buy good-quality jars of pickled
gherkins, onions, that sort of thing, you'll find that
they are usually preserved in spirit vinegar. When
you've eaten the pickles, use the vinegar for sauces

such as this.) Season with salt and pepper. Finely chop the shallots and add them too.

When ready to serve, slice your sausages and keep them warm under a low grill or in the oven. Place the sliced potatoes in a wire sieve and dip into the hot water to heat them through again. (The pot containing the hot water is now known as a *chauffante* in kitchen parlance. And while we're on the subject, the glass of wine you hand the cook every so often is called the *consolante*. Do not over-console, though, as burning the house down often dismays.)

Remove the potatoes, shake off the excess water and drop immediately into the vinaigrette in the bowl. Stir immediately, as the hot wet potatoes absorb so much of the sauce – which really is what makes it so special, despite the small number of ingredients. The combination of shallot and vinegar goes right to the heart of each slice of potato, rendering this dish unforgettable and unputdownable. Add the slices of hot sausage and the parsley, mix and serve.

You absolutely want to dicky it up a bit? Chop in some hard-boiled egg, serve on a bed of shredded cos, present it by moulding in a pastry ring, and shove a sprig of flat-leaf parsley on top if you want to push the boat out. But do you know what? It's delicious just as it is.

Spaghettini con aglio, olio e peperoncino

This is one of the simplest and cheapest of pasta dishes, using few – and readily available – ingredients. While on a trip to Tuscany recently, I ate it in a restaurant there and noticed a variant in the cooking of the garlic, the essential ingredient of this dish (apart from the pasta): the cloves were left whole. It is my interpretation of their dish that I now offer, rather than the way I have been making it for years, now since abandoned.

Spaghettini (Thinner than spaghetti; I prefer it for
    this recipe. Choose the best brand you can afford,
    and avoid generic supermarket el cheapo
    brands.)
1 chilli, seeded and chopped
Salt and black pepper
1 head of garlic
1 bunch of parsley

The difference in this recipe is that instead of the crushed, chopped and fried garlic that I used to use, this one uses whole garlic cooked and softened on the pan (when it is referred to as soft or sweet garlic). It provides an incredible oomph to the whole caboodle.

This recipe could not be simpler. The only 'complicated' bit comes in the preparation of the soft garlic – which could be quite 'cheffy', if you choose to take it down the roasting/tin-foil avenue. We'll just take the pedestrian crossing. Separate the cloves of garlic and place them, whole, in some gently simmering water. Remove the garlic after some ten minutes, allow to cool and then peel them. Transfer them to the pan containing the olive oil in which you've already been cooking the chilli and allow them to fry gently in this, letting them colour lightly but without burning.

When this is on the way, place a quantity of pasta in the same water (about half a packet will be sufficient for a starter portion for four), add a pinch of salt and bring it back to the boil. Being thinner, it will cook quite quickly, so remove a strand every now and then and taste it. When ready, drain, but leave a little of the cooking water in the pot. (This is an Italian trick that makes sure that the pasta remains piping hot but also imparts an indefinable something to all their sauces.)

Using tongs, transfer the pasta to the pan with the chilli, olive oil and garlic. Sprinkle with a little chopped parsley, adjust the seasoning and then transfer to hot plates. It's quick, it's utterly delicious and it looks great. Note, too, the complete absence of Parmesan cheese. This is not to keep costs down (as it irrefutably does) but is a question of taste. Italians do not serve Parmesan with seafood pasta dishes or with pasta containing chilli.

Hot chickpeas

This is a delicious recipe for what is essentially Moroccan street food. It is supremely simple to make and full of exotic and intoxicating flavours. The chickpeas can be made in advance; they will keep for around a week in the fridge in Tupperware, and can be eaten whenever required. If you can get a hold of some saffron, do use it, as it will bring a sublime and authentic flavour to the mix.

I enjoy making and eating this so much that it has become a weekly staple! Ideal for kicking off a meal or as party food – or, indeed, as an anytime snack. Ideal too for impressing girls – not for nothing are they called 'chick peas'.

2 tins of chickpeas
A little olive oil
1 onion
1 red onion
1 red pepper
1 teaspoon of ground cumin
A bunch of coriander
Salt and black pepper
Pinch of saffron (optional)

Drain the chickpeas but keep a little of their liquid back. (You can use dried chickpeas if you prefer, in which case retain a little of the cooking water. But be aware that you will need to soak them all night, changing the water several times, and then cook them for hours. There's nothing wrong with tinned chickpeas.)

Finely chop the onion and the red pepper. Heat a little of the olive oil in a saucepan and cook the onion and pepper for a few minutes. Then add the cumin, stir in well and allow to cook before adding the chickpeas and their liquid. Season, and add saffron if desired. Leave to simmer for thirty minutes. When ready, cut the red onion in half and slice into very thin half-circles. Stir these into the chickpeas. (The heat of the chickpeas will 'cook' them.)

When the mixture has cooled, put it in the fridge for at least an hour. This will improve the flavour. When ready to serve, reheat gently.

It can be eaten with grilled pitta bread or, preferably, Moroccan flatbread and should definitely be accompanied by April March singing Serge Gainbourg's 'Chick Habit'.

Spiced Moroccan carrots

This is a delicious salad, to be served either warm or cold. It benefits from being made the day before, leaving the flavours to infuse in the fridge. Bursting with flavour and goodness, it is often served as a prelude to a Moroccan meal but is equally good as a snack.

500g carrots, cut into batons
Pinch of paprika
Pinch of cumin
Small bunch of flat-leaf parsley
Small bunch of coriander
Juice of one quarter of a lemon
A little olive oil
Teaspoon of coriander seeds

Cook the carrots in boiling water until just al dente: a couple of minutes should do it. Drain them and then mix with the cumin, paprika, chopped parsley and coriander, and add lemon juice and olive oil to coat. Toast the coriander seeds in a pan without burning and add these too.

Place in a bowl and transfer to the fridge for two hours. Season with a little salt and serve at room temperature.

Thai roast pork salad

This is a great way of using up leftovers and is equally successful with roast beef, turkey or chicken. The sauce is truly delicious and the crispy-garlic-and-shallot topping not only sets it all off but is just one tasty element of the genius of Thai cooking.

Juice of one lime
Fresh coriander
Fresh mint
Sesame oil
Groundnut oil
Caster sugar
Soy sauce
Fish sauce
2 cloves of garlic
1 shallot
Slices of roast pork
Little Gem lettuce
1 packet fresh bean sprouts
1 bunch scallions, chopped
1 red chilli

Squeeze the juice of one lime into a bowl and add to it the roughly chopped mint and coriander.

Add one tablespoon each of peanut and sesame oil, one of soy sauce and one of fish sauce, and mix well. Finally, add one tablespoon of sugar.

Peel and slice the garlic; do the same with the shallot. Fry both in a little sesame oil until crisp and golden.

Cut the slices of roast pork into julienne strips and fry in a separate pan.

Mix the salad ingredients, including the sliced chilli, in the dressing and coat well; arrange on a plate.

Garnish with the hot pork strips and spoon a little of the shallot-and-garlic mixture on top. Garnish with more chopped coriander.

Do not be tempted to add more fish sauce than the quantity given. I once got lambasted in the street by a viewer fuming at my televisual generosity with the old *nam pla*. Knew what she was talking about, too. Since I've made you buy the stuff and given you this warning, here's a rather jolly similar recipe from Vietnam that I've always enjoyed.

Vietnamese beef salad

400g rump steak
1 red chilli
2 cloves of garlic
2 shallots
Cashew nuts (optional)

For the marinade:

1 tablespoon sesame oil
2 tablespoons groundnut oil
1 tablespoon Vietnamese fish sauce (nuoc mam)
1 tablespoon rice vinegar
1 tablespoon soy sauce
1 small piece grated ginger
3 tablespoons fresh lime juice
1 large tablespoon brown sugar (palm sugar, if available)

For the salad:

Various leaves – such as oak-leaf lettuce, Little Gem, rocket, peeled and seeded cucumber, bunch of scallions, papaya, mangetout, and herbs such as coriander, basil and fresh mint

Begin by making the marinade by mixing all the above ingredients together; add to the beef and leave for at least thirty minutes, reserving some of the marinade for later.

Pan-fry or barbecue the meat, cooking it no more than medium rare.

Assemble the ingredients for the salad in a bowl. Dice the papaya, julienne the mangetout and peel and seed the cucumber before slicing it thinly in half-circles. Chop the scallions. Mix the ingredients together with the three herbs, finely chopped.

Quickly fry the chopped red chilli, crushed garlic and chopped shallots all together in hot groundnut oil until crispy and add some chopped cashew nuts (if using). Off the heat, add some finely chopped coriander.

Assemble by plating the salad and sprinkling with some of the marinade. Slice the beef thinly and arrange on top. Sprinkle with the garlic-shallot mix and spoon over a little more of the marinade.

Bang bang chicken salad

I doubt very much if you've gone into a modern restaurant in the last ten years and not come across either Thai fishcakes or this one: Bang bang chicken salad. You've probably enjoyed it, and you've certainly wondered, owing to the name, what it was. Here's the recipe.

1 breast of chicken, skinless
Six scallions, chopped
1 or 2 Little Gem lettuce
1 cucumber
Groundnut oil
2 fiery red chillis
1 tablespoon rice wine
1 tablespoon brown sugar
1 tablespoon sesame oil
1 tablespoon sesame seeds
Small piece of fresh ginger
Peanut butter
60g beansprouts
2 carrots, grated

Place the breast of chicken in a pot with water and some of the chopped scallions. Allow to poach for about five minutes and then drain, refresh by holding under cold running water and shred the chicken.

Heat some peanut oil in a pan and quickly fry the chopped chillis, the sesame seeds and the sugar. After a minute, add the rice wine and a tablespoon of peanut butter. Remove from the heat and allow to cool.

Make the salad by mixing the rest of the scallions with the grated carrots and beansprouts. Arrange the Little Gem leaves on a plate and scatter the other ingredients around them. Top this with the shredded chicken and spoon the sauce over the top. Sprinkle with a julienne of cucumber that has been seeded, and finally some more toasted sesame seeds.

Tarts

I love tarts, me. All manner of tarts. I particularly hate that dopey expression 'Real men don't eat quiche' – such tommyrot. The only thing I don't like is the wet slop, microwaved into submission, that often passes for quiche in this country. However, fair enough, I have probably milked my favourite Alsace onion tart to death (and it featured in my other book, *Around Ireland with a Pan*), so here are two special favourites, both quite different.

A pissaladière of goat's cheese with onion, cherry tomatoes and courgettes

A *pissaladière* is one of those great Provençale favourites, gastronomically cognate with Italian pizza, since much of the region as far as Nice used to be part of Italy. This is a fancy version without the anchovies which traditionally form part of the recipe, though I've left the onions in. It's great for using up that goat's cheese you never got round to eating, or the cherry tomatoes which looked so inviting in the supermarket but you now can't think what to do with.

200g plain flour
Olive oil

Salted water
6 onions
Pinch of sugar
Goat's cheese, to crumble
10 cherry tomatoes
2 courgettes
Dill
Sprigs of thyme
Salt and pepper
Paprika or cayenne pepper, or piment d'espelette

Make a dough by combining the flour with olive oil until it begins to form a ball: bind with the water, cover in a bowl and leave to chill in the fridge for at least thirty minutes.

Cut the onions quite thickly and allow to cook gently in a little olive oil with the thyme until they are soft and transparent.

Slice the courgettes into batons and brush with olive oil before grilling on a hot grill pan for a few minutes until marked.

Roll out the dough into a 30cm tart mould: spread the base with the onion-and-thyme mix and place in the oven at 180 degrees.

Remove after ten minutes and add the cherry tomatoes whole, and the batons of courgettes. Crumble the goat's cheese over the top generously.

Return to the oven and cook for a further twenty minutes, or until the cheese has melted.

Remove from oven and sprinkle with a little paprika (or, if you can find it, *piment d'espelette*, the wonderful, mildly spicy chilli powder from the French side of the Basque country).

Parsley and Gruyère tart

Many years ago, a pastry chef who worked alongside me for many years made me this tart, or quiche. I was delighted with it, finding it fresh, light and invigorating, and it's been in my repertoire ever since. Since it contains a little crème fraiche (which can be replaced with some ordinary cream), it's a tad naughty from a budgetary point of view, but what the hey. Have it once in a blue moon. I made it for Christmas last year and my young son devoured it, declaring: 'Hey Dad, finally something that doesn't taste like crap.' Someone's been watching too much *Family Guy*.

This is one of those tarts which is a splendid example of an oven-to-table dish. It will never taste better (or look better) than when served straight from the oven, accompanied by a simple green salad. The filling, which is almost soufflé-like, will drop quite quickly, so dig in!

220g plain flour
100g unsalted butter
1 egg yolk
Sea salt and table salt
Black pepper
Nutmeg
Dollop of Dijon mustard (optional)

1 small bunch of parsley, chopped fine
50g Emmenthal or Gruyère, grated finely
4 tablespoons of crème fraiche and a little milk
4 eggs
5 tablespoons chilled water

For this tart, you will need a tart ring or mould, 25 to 30cm wide, and preferably with a removable base. You can grease this all over with a tiny knob of butter, using a little of the foil the butter came wrapped in. Let's begin by making the pastry.

First of all, leave the butter out for a while until it is at room temperature and soft. If unsalted butter is too expensive then use ordinary butter, but be careful when seasoning the dough. Mix the butter with the egg yolk, then add the water tablespoon by tablespoon (together with a little salt, if you have used unsalted butter).

Add to this the flour, a little at a time, until you have a ball of dough which doesn't stick to the bowl or to your fingers. Put this to one side in the fridge for at least thirty minutes, with a damp cloth covering the bowl.

Heat the oven to 180 degrees at this point. To make the filling for the tart, beat the eggs as for an omelette, then add the eggs and a splash of milk. Grate the Gruyère (once again old and tired cheese, even with hard edges, is perfect for this) and add to the mix, followed by the finely chopped parsley. Season with salt and pepper, taste to make sure it's adequately seasoned, and return to the dough in the fridge.

Roll this out quite thinly and add to your pastry ring, allowing the pastry to fall over the sides of the ring. Here, you can spread the base of the pastry with a thin layer of mustard, or you can ignore me and just not bother, if you're not a huge fan of mustard.

Pour the parsley and Gruyère mixture into the rolled-out pastry. (It should come about two-thirds of the way up the side.) Make sure the cheese is completely covered by the egg and cream. Then trim the edges of the pastry so that it fits snugly into the pastry ring.

Pop into the oven and allow to cook for about thirty minutes. Keep an eye on it, and turn it regularly so that the filling cooks evenly. When the mixture has risen and begun to crack, it should be perfectly cooked; the pastry should have come away from the sides of the ring.

Piperata vasca or biperrada

Piperade is known throughout the Basque country, especially in the French part, where it features the traditional *Piment d'espelette* (mentioned earlier in the *pissaladière* recipe (page 75), a warm and pungent chilli, yet at the same time very mild but toothsome – unlike its fiery cousins from South America, the West Indies and Africa. In the absence of the *Piment d'espelette*, one can replace it with a little paprika – not quite the same, but suitable.

This is essentially a vegetarian-friendly stew and a close relative of ratatouille, but with the addition of eggs. I am prompted to include it because it reminds me of the late Keith Floyd and his hilarious attempts to make it while being berated by an irate local. (That clip can be seen on *youtube.com* and is well worth a watch.)

A family favourite and pleasant supper dish, it can also be reheated the next day and is even more delicious then!

1 or 2 onions
2 cloves of garlic
1 red pepper
1 green pepper
4 tomatoes

Olive oil
6 eggs
Pinch of piment d'espelette or paprika
Salt and black pepper
Fresh parsley
Basil

Begin by cooking the sliced onions and the crushed garlic in the oil for around five minutes. Slice the peppers lengthwise into thin strips and cook for a further five minutes.

Now skin the tomatoes by plunging them into boiling water, then peel, chop and deseed them. Add these to the onion-and-pepper mixture.

Beat the eggs as for an omelette and season with salt, pepper, paprika and chopped basil. Add to the tomato mixture, or *piperade*, and stir in slowly, as for scrambled eggs. Alternatively, you can break the eggs in whole, covering the whites in *piperade*, which will cook them, and allowing the yolks to peep through. When almost set, sprinkle with chopped parsley and a little *piment d'espelette* or paprika if desired.

A *piperade* would normally include the region's speciality, *Jambon de Bayonne*, but I've left it out for reasons of cost and to make this recipe one for the vegetarians. But feel free to add it or some other ham similar to it, if the purse allows and you are not of the vegetarian faith.

Ceviche

On TV recently, I saw Jamie Oliver in America talking about ceviche with some Mexicans. It has prompted me to include this, resurrected from one of my many hard drives. Clearly my recipe is much better than his.

Ceviche is one of the most famous marinades of South America: its origins are said to be in Ecuador and Peru, but it certainly has antecedents in the cuisines of Spain and Portugal.

It is best used with white fish, as it changes the colour of the raw fish as soon as it comes in contact with it. It is also excellent with firm, meaty fishes such as red snapper. Naturally, we don't need to go seeking out rare and exotic fish: we live on an island, after all, and many inexpensive and suitable fish can be sourced locally.

Once the marinade has been applied, the fish can be eaten 'as is' or rolled up in a warm corn tortilla. The marinade takes about five minutes to prepare, but it is best to make it at least six hours in advance.

1 kg fish filets, such as red snapper, cut into chunks
Juice of 1 lime
Juice of 1 lemon

1 red onion, finely chopped
2 tomatoes, skinned and diced
1 red chilli, finely chopped
Pinch of salt
Fresh oregano
Fresh coriander
Pinch of cayenne pepper
Tortillas (optional)
1 avocado, diced (optional)

Mix all the ingredients together and leave to combine for six hours. When ready to eat, spoon over the chunks of fish.

If desired, place on a warm tortilla, top with avocado dice and then roll up and eat! As the meerkats say, *simples*!

Chicken salad with fromage frais dressing

Looking to reduce cost – or your waistline? Starving yourself is no answer, but you could try this salad instead. I wasn't going to include it but then made something very like it the other day and it was quite the hit, the dressing in particular.

1 lettuce
1 leg of chicken
1 lemon
2 red chillis
2 waxy potatoes
30g feta cheese
1 scallion
3 black olives per person
Salt and black pepper
1 head of garlic
1 tub fromage frais
Pinch of paprika

Bring some water to the boil with a pinch of salt, one chilli (split), and one crushed clove of garlic, and reduce the heat to simmer. Add the leg of chicken and leave until cooked (around twenty to thirty minutes). You could use far costlier breast of chicken, but frankly it won't be as tasty, and it won't work as well. Start using those legs! They are far better value, and far more succulent.

Crush another clove of garlic and add this to the fromage frais with a little salt and pepper, the grated zest of one lemon and the juice of half the lemon, plus a little chopped chilli.

Boil the potatoes, cool and slice them, then grill them on a grill pan. Season to taste. Assemble the salad: the washed leaves, diced feta, chopped olives and scallion, cut diagonally. Do not dress until the last minute. (The salad, not you.) Of course, if you really don't like olives, you can leave these out, but from the point of view of colour and taste, it would be a shame not to include them.

Remove the chicken from the water and strip of all its flesh using a sharp knife.

Mix the salad ingredients with the fromage frais dressing and place each portion in a bowl or on a plate. Arrange some of the chicken on top and surround with slices of grilled potato. To serve, add a dollop of the dressing on top, and sprinkle with a little paprika.

Chiquetaille of salt cod with chilled cucumber

Now here's a curio: you may have seen those long strips of salt cod hanging up in your local fishmonger. Salting is a method of preserving fish for long periods, particularly for navies; it is particularly associated with Portugal. They say that that country has a recipe for salt cod for every day of the year, and there are also myriad recipes from Catalonia; the classic recipe is of course, *brandade*, from the south of France. Here's a delicious take on this adaptable fish recipe from the French West Indies. Although salt cod is not cheap in this country, fortunately a little goes a long way – and you don't have to worry about it going off!

800g salt cod
1 cucumber
1 small white onion
1 sprig of fresh thyme
4 cloves of garlic
1 tablespoon chopped parsley
2 tablespoons chopped scallions
3 limes
3 shallots
1 small red chilli

Olive oil
1 aubergine
1 sweet potato

It's a good idea to begin the prep the day before by grilling the piece of salt cod on both sides until it's slightly burnt, then soaking it in a large quantity of cold water. Change this water after one hour, then leave to soak all night.

When you're ready to start cooking, immerse the salt cod in boiling water for two minutes. Turn off the heat and leave in the water to go cold. These two techniques – the overnight soaking and the plunging into boiling water – remove the excess salt used to preserve the cod.

Drain the cod, then remove the skin and bones using the back of a knife. Make sure you get rid of them all. Flake all of the cod – this is the meaning of the Creole word *'chiquetaille'*.

Chop the shallots, garlic and onion into very small dice. Finely chop the parsley and add to the onions, then add the chopped scallion and the juice of the limes. Mix all of this with the flaked cod.

Now add three spoonfuls of olive oil plus the finely chopped thyme and chilli. Put the mixture in the fridge.

Wash and peel the cucumber, cut it lengthwise and

remove the middle section containing the seeds. Cut it into thin slices and put it in the fridge.

Slice the aubergine into rounds, rub them all over with olive oil and grill on both sides until coloured and quite soft. Allow to cool.

Using a pastry ring, assemble the *chiquetaille* by placing a layer of chilled cucumber on the bottom followed by a layer of the cod mix, a slice of aubergine, more cod, then a thin slice of sweet potato and finally a good layer of the cod once more on top. Garnish with some freshly chopped coriander and a final twist of lime juice.

Keep cool until ready to serve and remove the ring at the last minute.

Brandade de morue

We can't *not* give the recipe for *brandade de morue* – the classic way to serve salt cod. (*'Morue'* is the French word for cod, once salted, as opposed to *'cabillaud'*, which refers to fresh cod.) *Brandade* turns up frequently in fancy restaurants these days as a small quenelle next to a larger serving of a much nobler fish, but before chefs got their hands on it, it was a classic beginning to a meal or a main course in its own right. Here's a tried-and-trusted recipe for it.

> *800g salt cod*
> *250ml milk*
> *2 cloves of garlic*
> *1 lemon*
> *250ml of quality olive oil, preferably extra virgin*
> *Salt, pepper and nutmeg*

Again, the salt cod must be left to soak in water overnight, for at least twenty-four hours, and this water should be changed several times.

The salt cod should be drained and then left under cold running water for a few minutes. Then place it in cold water, bring to the boil and allow to simmer for fifteen minutes in a pot of water; then drain again. Using your fingers and a knife, remove the skin, along with any bones. Keep the fish warm.

Flake the salt cod and use a pestle and mortar to pound the fish with the garlic until it forms a thick paste. At the same time, combine the olive oil with the milk and heat over a low flame. Add the cod-and-garlic mix to this, and stir together until it has a smooth, creamy consistency.

Take off the heat, check the seasoning and add a little grated nutmeg.

Traditionally, *brandade de morue* is served hot with stale bread (which can be made into croutons) and black olives. But it can also be served cold with a selection of Mediterranean leaves.

MAIN COURSES:
MEAT AND POULTRY

Colombo of chicken

I'm going to start off this section with something which is quite exotic but also fun and rewarding to make. It's a curry from the French West Indies, known as a 'colombo'. This curry is eaten all over the islands of Martinique and Guadeloupe in myriad guises, and will out-curry anything you can get from your nearest curry outlet, and save you a few bob to boot. This one is made with our old friend the chicken, but the inhabitants of the French West Indies use anything from goat to flying fish. The key thing here is the colombo paste, the origins of which can be found in the cooking habits of the indentured labourers brought there in the early part of the twentieth century – and which makes it quite different from the curries we know and love in this part of the world.

2 chicken breast fillets, skin on, bone in
200g new potatoes
1 onion
4 cloves of garlic
Small piece of fresh ginger
1 tablespoon cumin seeds
1 green chilli
Small tub of natural yoghurt
350ml chicken stock

Small bag of spinach
1 bunch of coriander
Handful of parsley
1 teaspoon of coriander seeds
1 tablespoon groundnut oil
1 lemon

For the colombo paste:

2 cloves of garlic
1 red chilli
1 teaspoon each of turmeric, ground coriander and mustard powder

Make the colombo paste by crushing the garlic and chopping and mashing the chilli, then combine this with the other ingredients.

Begin by frying the chicken in a little oil. When it's browned all over, add the chopped onion, followed by the crushed garlic. Cook for another minute, then add the potatoes, which you will have quartered, plus the finely chopped garlic and then all the spices and chilli.

Cook this for another five minutes and reduce the heat. Incorporate the colombo paste off the heat and stir well. Add all the stock, bring to the boil and allow to simmer. Wash and chop the spinach and, when the chicken is cooked through (it'll take about twenty minutes), add this. Off the heat, stir in the yoghurt and chopped coriander. Add a squeeze of lemon and serve immediately. How hard is that?

A simple chicken stir-fry

Here's a good recipe for a powerful and tasty stir-fry. If you prepare it the night before, you can microwave or reheat it for a simple lunch the next day. If you shop in your local Asian supermarket, you can pick up the ingredients quite cheaply.

4 breasts of chicken, cut into strips
3 cloves of garlic, finely chopped
1 teaspoon coriander seeds
1 teaspoon Sichuan pepper
1 bag of bok choi
6 shiitake mushrooms
1 carrot
1 head of broccoli, separated into florets
Finely chopped fresh ginger
1 bunch of scallions
Groundnut oil
Sesame oil
1 bunch of fresh coriander
120ml mirin (a rice-based Japanese ingredient)
120ml Japanese soy sauce
3 tablespoons sake
2 tablespoons brown sugar

Begin by making the marinade: combine the sake, soy sauce, mirin and sugar in a large bowl and place the chicken strips in it. Leave for at least thirty minutes (or prepare the day before).

Peel the carrot and slice into long strips with a vegetable peeler. Slice the scallions at an angle. Trim the bok choi and shred the leaves. Remove the mushroom stalks and slice the heads into strips.

Heat a wide frying pan or wok and pour four tablespoons of groundnut oil into it. Drain the chicken through a sieve, keeping the marinade, and then mix the chopped garlic and ginger through it.

When the oil is hot and beginning to smoke (the flame should be quite high), toss in the chicken and begin to cook it, tossing it every so often. After a couple of minutes, and when it is coloured on each side, remove from the pan and set to one side.

Now throw in the ribbons of carrot with a little sesame oil. Cook quickly, then add the bok choi, shiitake strips, broccoli and scallions. Crush the pepper and coriander seeds (with a pestle and mortar or the back of a spoon) and throw these in too, before returning the chicken, with its juices and marinade, to the pan.

Leave the ingredients to combine for a few minutes. Toss in some chopped coriander leaves and garnish each plateful with the rest.

Belly pork with noodles

Belly of pork, like shank of lamb, confit of duck, and monkfish and tuna before it, is one of those cheap ingredients which chefs have seized upon to make wonderful dishes out of very little and maximise their profits. Nothing shameful about that, but it has the unfortunate effect of pushing up the price of the ingredient in question, as we want to re-create the cheffy dishes at home. For the moment, belly pork remains supremely afford-able, but stay on good terms with your friendly local butcher. Here's a terrific recipe using it.

*Pork belly (100g per person), cut into a small
    rectangle*
Juice of two limes
Sea salt and black pepper
4 scallions
1 chilli
Bunch of coriander
Groundnut oil
1 packet medium egg noodles

For the honey marinade:

5 teaspoons honey
3 teaspoons Japanese soy sauce
4 cloves of garlic

1 small piece of fresh ginger
Pinch of chilli flakes
Pinch each of ground coriander, cumin, cinnamon,
    ginger and turmeric

Begin by mixing all the marinade ingredients together into a paste, then lengthen with some water. Pour over the pork pieces and put to one side. Heat the oven to 180 degrees.

Transfer the pork pieces to a roasting tin after half an hour of marinating, cover with tinfoil and place in the oven for around an hour and a half.

When the meat is tender, remove it and place on a warm, deep plate, leaving the sauce in the oven tray. Taste the sauce and adjust the seasoning if necessary, adding a little salt, pepper or soy sauce. If it needs to be thickened, reduce over a medium flame on the hob.

Cook the noodles: drop them into boiling water, drain when almost cooked and return to the heat, mixing with the scallions and fresh chillies, both julienned. Season to taste.

At the same time, heat a little oil in the pan and fry the pork pieces until crispy all over. Serve the noodles, arranging the belly pork on top and adding the sauce and some of the lime juice.

Grilled lamb chops with a warm chickpea, lemon and olive dressing

Here's a really simple lamb dish, but one which looks good and can be held in reserve for a dinner where you are looking to impress your other half or someone equally important (that is, not bank managers who have fallen from grace). It features the return of our chum the chickpea, in the guise of a salsa, and requires no other foil, really. While the lamb chops are not the cheapest cut, the supermarkets these days often offer half-price bargains on meat. You should be looking to pounce at about 6.30 in the evening.

8 lamb centre-loin chops
Olive oil
Handful of fresh sage leaves
Squeeze of lemon juice
50g black olives, finely chopped
1 tin of chickpeas
1 avocado, diced
1 punnet of cherry tomatoes, halved
100g broccoli sprouts
Salt and pepper

In a bowl, mix a couple of tablespoons of oil, chopped sage and lemon juice. Add to this the lamb chops and mix well. Season the lamb with sea salt and ground black pepper.

Mix the chickpeas in a bowl with the olives, tomatoes and avocado.

Dress with olive oil and lemon juice, season and mix well. Place in a saucepan and leave over a very low heat.

On a grill pan, over a high heat, grill the chops for a few minutes each side, or longer if you prefer. When ready, remove the saucepan from the heat, mix well, then add the broccoli sprouts. (If you can't get broccoli, use beansprouts.)

Casserole of Irish beef with Celtic beer and roasted root vegetables

You can judge the culinary mood of the country by the number of slow cookers now being offered for sale in the likes of Asda, Lidl, TK Maxx and elsewhere. Stews and similar dishes are back in again! In fact, somebody in the factory in *Coronation Street* got a birthday present of one recently, showing just how in touch the writers are with their viewers. Actually, I recommend that you pick up a tagine instead: the ones in Ikea are really cool, perform much the same task as a slow cooker, and the base, while not being used for the aromatic delicacies of the Maghreb, can instead be used for *poule au pot, coq au vin*, Irish stew or cassoulet, not to mention just sautéing potatoes for family meals. (Then again, you already have your very large pot.) So here's a hearty Irish beef stew, celebrating our vegetables and using one of our Irish beers forbye!

1 kg diced stewing steak
10g flour
1 litre beef stock
2 bay leaves
1 bunch of thyme

100g button mushrooms
2 onions
2 carrots
2 parsnips
1 turnip
A little olive oil
Unsalted butter
1 bottle of Irish beer (330ml)
Sea salt
Cracked black pepper
Italian leaf parsley

There are plenty of ingredients, but this recipe couldn't be simpler. Begin by leaving the beef to marinate in the beer overnight with the bay leaves and a little thyme.

When ready to cook, heat the oven to 160 degrees. Remove the beef from the marinade and sauté over a medium heat in a mixture of a little butter and a tablespoon of olive oil – that most Irish of combinations.

Brown the pieces of meat all over, then sprinkle with a little flour and leave to cook for another couple of minutes to 'singe' them – that is, cooking out the flour and amalgamating the juices. Remove from the pot and keep in a bowl.

Slice the onions (or cut into quarters if preferred) and place in the same pot, adding a little more oil and butter if needed. Stir over a medium heat for a few minutes until they soften.

Return the beef to the pot with the onions and add to this the beef and then its marinade, including the bay and thyme. Bring to the boil, add the stock, bring back to the boil, and then reduce to simmer.

Cover with the lid of the pot and place in the oven. Cook for two hours, adding the mushrooms halfway through the cooking time.

Prep all the root vegetables by peeling them and cutting them into irregular, bite-sized pieces. Blanch them in boiling water, drain and refresh, then toss them in olive oil, chopped thyme, and salt and pepper, and place, uncovered, in the same oven to roast and colour. Remove when ready.

When the beef is tender, remove the casserole from the oven and place over a medium flame. Further reduce the liquid if required, to thicken the sauce and coat the meat. Add the root vegetables to this; mix in well and correct the seasoning.

Garnish with Italian leaf parsley.

Poule au pot

I often watch *Saturday Kitchen* on the BBC; when it doesn't have the more outrageous (and therefore annoying) chefs on, it's a good watch – perfect with a late breakfast and a source of good tips. Recently, they showed a clip of Rick Stein going round France and discovering *poule au pot*. This dish, famous for being the one that Henri IV of France wanted all of his subjects to have each and every Sunday, suits our purposes perfectly because it is cheap, hearty, intensely flavoursome, multifaceted and satisfying. It is often served with three condiments on the side – gherkins (cornichons), sea salt and mustard – and rarely with potatoes but often with rice, which mops up the white sauce (made from its broth) admirably. In addition, the broth is often served as a first course. I have never seen it served with *sauce gribiche*, an excellent caper-based sauce more often partnered with calf's head, in the manner Mr Stein described, but perhaps he's right and I'm wrong. It looked very nice, in any case. Where we definitely part company, though, is in his use of a chicken rather than the *poule* of the dish's name which should be a hen or boiling fowl. These boiling fowls can be found in good butchers or in Asian supermarkets, usually for the price of a song. There's a restaurant in Paris called Poule au Pot which serves it until about five in the morning. They claim that the Rolling Stones used to go there. Here's what to do.

For the bird:

One boiling fowl (and ask for the giblets too)
4 carrots
2 turnips (those lovely little purple ones would suit)
1 leek
1 bouquet garni
400g of easy-cook rice

For the white sauce:

50g plain flour
50g butter
About a litre of the water in which the fowl was boiled
Piment d'espelette or paprika

The condiments:

One small jar of cornichons
One small jar of Dijon mustard
One ramekin of sea salt

The stuffing:

250g minced pork or sausage meat
Slices of stale bread
The giblets from the boiling fowl
4 chicken livers

100ml of milk
2 eggs
1 shallot
3 cloves of garlic
Thyme, bay and parsley

For the stuffing, soak the bread in the milk and chop up the livers and the giblets very finely, and all the garlic and shallot. Mix this with the eggs and then the bread, having drained the excess milk. Finally add the sausage meat, using either freshly bought minced pork or, preferably, the meat from good coarse sausages. This needs to be mixed thoroughly with the bay, thyme and parsley; then place it inside the bird and sew the opening together. If you're not a dab hand at sewing – I'm not – a strategically placed half an onion will do fine, keeping the stuffing inside.

Now start cooking the bird. Because you've gone and got a boiling fowl or hen, this is going to take a while to cook. If you use a chicken, you will need to shorten the cooking time considerably. Place the fowl in your very large pot (you know exactly where it is by now) and add the bouquet garni and a pinch of salt. Cover with water, bring to the boil and allow to simmer for a couple of hours – these are tough, you know. Skim frequently. After this time, add the carrots, turnips and leek – cleaned, trimmed, peeled but whole –

and leave to simmer for at least another hour. When done, remove from the heat and leave the ensemble to cool.

Chop all the onion, then skim off some of the fat floating on top of the liquid in which you've cooked the bird and pour this into a frying pan. Now gently fry the onions in that. When it begins to colour, add the rice, then ladle stock from your pot onto that as you go along, until the rice is cooked, very like a paella or risotto.

Finally, begin the sauce. Make a classic roux by melting the butter in a saucepan, adding the flour and allowing to cook for a few minutes to avoid any 'floury' taste. Add more stock to this over a low heat (the fact that the stock is hot should avoid lumps, but either whisk with gusto or stir with a wooden spoon with vim). When the sauce has thickened, remove from the heat, stir in the egg yolks, season with salt and *piment d'espelette* or paprika. You are now ready to serve.

The hen is cut up into pieces, its stuffing served alongside it, surrounded by the wonderful vegetables. On the side, the rice, and to top it, your unctuous sauce, made from the stock you created from the long cooking of the bird. Serve with the sea salt, gherkins and mustard.

Chicken stew Basque style

There was no real toil in the last dish but it does demand a great deal of time and attention, which is what real cooking is all about. It is these hearty classic dishes that satisfy appetites and make the most of very little but, as clever ol' Henri IV intended, it was for a Sunday lunch and could be prepared the night before. We won't always have time for dishes like this – though we should make time for healthier and happier living – so here is a quicker dish which I've enjoyed for more than three decades. This is one of those canteen staples – I've even had it on the ferry from Ireland to Brittany – and it's a real crowd-pleaser, including for kids.

4 chicken legs
Olive oil or goose fat
2 red and 2 green peppers (seeded and sliced)
*1 thick slice of Bayonne ham (or any other good-
    quality, thick ham)*
2 chopped onions
Glass of white wine
2 cloves of garlic, roughly chopped
1 tin of chopped tomatoes or six fresh ones
*1 'Espelette' chilli (if not available, use a teaspoon
    of paprika)*

Salt
Spoonful of crème fraiche (optional)
Handful of chopped parsley

Begin by warming the olive oil or goose fat in a frying pan. Gently cook the onions and garlic together for about ten to fifteen minutes until soft. Remove from the pan and transfer to a large pot.

Heat the pan again using the same oil and place the chicken legs, skin side down, to brown. Do both sides for about five minutes and salt them while doing so. Then transfer these to the pot without the fat.

Cut the ham into little lardons and quickly fry these in the pan: add the wine to this, allow to reduce, and then pour the lot into the pot.

Add the tomatoes to this mixture, then the peppers, and finally the paprika. Bring it to a simmer and then cover and allow to cook for around forty-five minutes.

When ready to serve, remove the chicken and allow the sauce to reduce and thicken over a high heat. Remove from the heat, stir in a little crème fraiche and the parsley, adjust the seasoning and serve poured over the chicken.

This is best served with rice but will go equally well with boiled potatoes or mash.

Grilled bacon chop with a ragout of broad beans and mustard cabbage

Like the belly pork dish on page 99, cuts like bacon chops are becoming popular once more and easy to find. I love dishes like this, especially when partnered with cabbage – possibly my favourite vegetable. Here's a lovely recipe to marry these two fabulous ingredients; it's made even better with the pungency of mustard and bulked up with broad beans.

1 bacon chop per person
1 cabbage, shredded
1 jar Dijon mustard
1 glass dry white wine
Small bunch fresh rosemary
Salt and black pepper
Fennel seeds
1 clove of garlic
1 lemon
150g unsalted butter
10 baby onions
1 tin broad beans
A little olive oil

Begin by marinating the chop in a little olive oil with pepper, crushed garlic and chopped rosemary.

Gently braise the cabbage in a little white wine over a low heat. Toast some fennel seeds (in a dry pan) and add these to the cabbage.

Melt a little butter in a pan, add the peeled young onions and cook until lightly coloured. Moisten with a glass of water and simmer for ten minutes until soft.

Add the broad beans to this, season, and then, over a low heat, stir in some more butter and allow to thicken.

Remove the bacon chop from the marinade and cook on a grill pan for four or five minutes on each side, depending on thickness.

Stir a little mustard into the cabbage and check the seasoning.

In a deep plate, spoon in the ragout of beans and then place some of the cabbage on top.

Place the grilled bacon chop on top of the cabbage and serve immediately.

Quick tagine of kefta

I love the cooking of North Africa, especially that of Morocco – as is evidenced by the number of recipes from that country that I offer here. But it's hard to find such dishes that are quick (even if they are generally cheap), and even Moroccans are known not to have patience for the laborious demands of their own cuisine. Here, then, is one of the quicker and simpler tagines, made with kefta or minced beef, formed into meatballs. Everybody loves meatballs, right?

1 onion
1 stick of celery
1 clove of garlic
1 tin of chopped tomatoes
1 red pepper
1 green pepper
350g minced beef
Spices such as ground coriander, cumin, turmeric,
*   cinnamon and ginger*
Salt and black pepper
Olive oil
Small bunch of parsley
Small bunch of coriander
1 egg (optional)

Slice the onion finely and crush and chop the garlic. Chop the celery and slowly fry all three in a little olive oil. Seed the peppers and slice thinly, and add these to the tagine (if you have one) or simply a pan.

While the vegetables are softening, mix the meat with a little oil, salt, pepper and ground coriander.

Roll the mince (kefta) into small meatballs with your palms and fry gently in a pan until coloured all over.

Return to the vegetable mix and add a teaspoon each of cumin, coriander, turmeric and ginger – or whichever of these spices you have to hand. Allow to cook for a few minutes, then add the tin of chopped tomatoes and stir well. Season with salt and pepper and allow to simmer.

Now transfer the meatballs to this mixture and allow to cook in the sauce. If you can cover the tagine (or pot) with a lid, so much the better.

When ready to serve, stir in some freshly chopped parsley and coriander. The addition of an egg, added (and cooked) in the centre of the mix five minutes before serving, is quite delicious. Serve piping hot with flatbread or pitta.

Turkey

The Italians and French have long known that a turkey is not just for Christmas. In fact, turkey steaks or escalopes are an exciting and healthy way to eat this bird, as little cooking time is involved, and they have none of the heaviness associated with festive recipes. Lately, turkey legs have been appearing in supermarkets; these lend themselves to a variety of recipes and preparations, for very little outlay. Unfortunately, it seems that the supermarkets have already caught on to this, and the price per leg has increased by around 80 cents over the last year alone. It's still a bargain, though, and I have tried many different recipes for it that were out of the ordinary, yet cheap to realise. This one, I feel, was the most successful.

Mechoui of leg of turkey

A *mechoui* is one of the loveliest of Moroccan dishes, usually made with lamb and traditionally associated with some of the more important festivals in the Islamic religious calender. It involves making a rich paste of butter and cumin, slicing into the flesh and rubbing the paste all over the meat and right inside it, then leaving it to work its magic on the joint before a slow roasting. I've adapted the original recipe for the leg of turkey: it works incredibly well, and provides you with a wholesome and cheap treat for a more elaborate weekend dinner or lunch.

> *2 legs of turkey (This should be enough for four people; if they're really hungry gorbs, allow a leg per person. This isn't going to break the bank, but be advised that there is a lot of eating on these.)*

To make the pommade (paste) for each leg:

> *50g butter*
> *3 cloves of garlic*
> *2 teaspoons ground cumin*
> *3 teaspoons ground coriander*
> *1 teaspoon paprika*
> *2 teaspoons sea salt*

To start, you need to cut deep slits into both sides of the leg, almost to the bone. Heat your oven to 220 degrees.

Have your butter at room temperature and mix with the crushed garlic, all the spices and half a teaspoon of sea salt until a very smooth paste is formed. Use your fingers to rub this all over the leg of turkey, deep into the slits and all over the flesh.

Then put it into a roasting tin and place in the oven for ten minutes, keeping an eye on it, as you don't want the butter to burn. Take it out of the oven, baste it with the juices that have formed, turn the oven down to around 160 degrees and place the leg back in the oven. Leave to slow roast for about three hours, though it may not need even that much, but do turn it and baste it again every thirty minutes. The turkey is ready when the meat is falling off the bone. A nice touch, I find, is to toast some cumin seeds in a pan and add them to the turkey for its last ten minutes in the oven. This *mechoui* is served with ground cumin and the rest of the sea salt on the side. This is hearty, festive stuff, so you may want to serve it with something relatively simple to mop up those juices – such as saffron potatoes, rice, spinach or grilled courgettes.

Escalopes of turkey with gremolata

Turkey steaks are simple to cook. At their most basic, you can simply grill them on a griddle pan and eat them with a little mustard for a quick, plain meal, or you can make a sauce to go with them. In any case, they cook much faster than chicken fillets and provide you with a nutritious meal in no time. I like their freshness and lightness (the less you cook them, the lighter and more easy to digest they will be) and can think of no better accompaniment to them than the Italian mix called *gremolata*.

2 turkey steaks per person
1 bag of spinach
3 cloves of garlic
1 bunch of parsley
Olive oil
1 lemon
Salt and black pepper

Gremolata is a cinch: you just need to finely chop all the parsley, crush the garlic, zest the lemon and mix everything together. Place in a bowl with a pinch of salt and a twist of black pepper and leave in the fridge for at least thirty minutes. *Gremolata* is traditionally served with osso bucco and should always be made fresh. It combines extremely well with fish of all sorts and is equally at home with grilled turkey escalopes.

To cook the turkey, heat your griddle pan, toss all the turkey steaks in a little olive oil, season with salt and black pepper and then grill them on the pan. To do this nicely, use the method called 'ten past ten', where the escalope is placed at an angle corresponding to ten on one side of the clock and then is angled to the two o'clock position. This is how you achieve that nice criss-cross effect. Repeat on the other side. When ready, serve with blanched spinach tossed in olive oil, place the grilled escalopes on top and sprinkle generously with *gremolata*.

Cassoulet

I mentioned cassoulet in the introduction, and we simply have to make it. It suits all the circumstances of our modern world and it comes from a time and a place where there was little save the fat of the land, and nothing, but nothing, was wasted. Even its very name – cassoulet – is reputed to be connected to the French verb *casser* (to break), reflecting the breaking of the fourteen layers of breadcrumbs that allegedly go into it. Hardly yuppie fare but so relevant to today – so keep those breadcrumbs! The dish itself is a thing of joy, full of sumptuous ingredients like sausage and goose fat and duck – the aforementioned fat of the land, so to speak – and demands time in its preparation and time in its eating. It's the king of bean dishes.

There is a lot of meat in this recipe, which is an authentic one, but should it not suit your needs – or budget – leave out the more expensive meats, such as goose. Try to have some chunks of pork and some Toulouse sausages or coarse Italian sausages in it at least, as well as some of the cheap pork hocks or bacon joints. Remember, a dish like this will get tastier each time you reheat it, so it should keep you satisfied for days.

500g dried haricot beans
Bouquet garni
1 carrot, cut into rounds
1 onion, sliced
1 clove of garlic, crushed

Meats:

120g belly pork
1 small tin of goose fat
1 small tin of confit of goose
1 hock of pork
1 bacon joint, around 200g
4 Toulouse sausages (or a coarse Italian sausage, which is often easier to find)
3 carrots
1 onion
1 clove of garlic
Lots of breadcrumbs

If you're using dried beans, the best thing is to soak them overnight or the day before in plenty of water and change the water several times.

When ready to commence cooking – that is, three hours before you're going to eat it – place the drained beans in Old Faithful (the very large pot) and cover with water. Add to this the belly pork, carrot, onion and garlic. Season with salt and pepper.

Bring to the boil, reduce the heat and leave to simmer for about ninety minutes.

When the beans are almost ready, cut all your meats, except the Toulouse sausages, into chunks and brown them all over in some goose fat. When this is done, add the sausages and brown those too, before adding the goose confit. (If you can't get that, confit of duck will do instead.) Chop all the vegetables – the carrot, onion and garlic – and add them to the meats.

When the beans are ready, drain half the water but retain the other half. Add this water and the beans to the meats and allow to simmer for a further thirty minutes. Transfer this to a large casserole (the bottom of your Ikea tagine will do), arranging the meat and beans in the bottom of the pan until it's full. Then sprinkle with a layer of breadcrumbs, pop into the oven (around 190 degrees) and brown this first layer of breadcrumbs. Tradition requires that this is done thirteen or fourteen times, but there is no need to go to those lengths. However, as a nod to that tradition, you might do it two or three times, for the craic. Moisten with any leftover juices as you go along, and adjust the seasoning, if necessary. When ready to eat, layer with one final covering of breadcrumbs and then serve when suitably golden.

Note: cassoulet does not have any tomatoes or cheese in the authentic recipe, and no herbs, apart from the bouquet garni.

Grilled spatchcocked chicken with Moroccan spices

When the demands of time and work do not allow for elaborate and time-consuming cooking, I like to be able to put something together to eat that is both tasty and hassle-free. This is never more important than when friends might drop in unexpectedly and are invited to stay to dinner.

For several weeks now, I have been preparing grilled chicken in the following way, both for myself and, a couple of times, for a small gathering of hungry chums. The recipe could not be easier or quicker, but it is also cheap, satisfying and colourful – and filled with the heady smells of North African cooking.

This is a dish in two parts: preparing the chicken and preparing the fantastic Moroccan mix of spices which is called *ras el-hanout* – an Arabic expression which means 'the top of the shop' (the best mix of spices the shopkeeper has to offer). *Ras el-hanout* can consist of anything from five to twenty-five spices; it reflects the conquests made over time by the Arabs, as they picked up a local spice or two in the countries they invaded on their way to the Maghreb. Typically, the mix contains ground coriander, cumin, nutmeg, turmeric, cloves, cinammon and cayenne pepper; more refined variants feature dried rose petals or rosebuds. Here's the basic recipe.

For the ras el-hanout:

3 teaspoons ground cinammon
3 teaspoons ground coriander
6 teaspoons ground nutmeg
2 teaspoons ground black pepper
1 teaspoon ground cloves
2 teaspoons ground cumin
2 teaspoons ground ginger
2 teaspoons ground turmeric
2 teaspoons ground cardamom
2 teaspoons ground chilli or cayenne pepper or paprika

Mix all the spices together and store in a jar. It's wonderful with all kinds of tagines and most meats. You can grind all the ingredients yourself if you feel so inclined, and you can also add similar quantities of lavender, allspice, the aforementioned dried rosebuds and white pepper, if you like. One thing is for sure: this blend will be far better than any ready-mixed 'Moroccan seasoning' you might spy on a supermarket shelf.

For the grilled chicken:

1 plump chicken
1 quantity ras el-hanout

6 garlic gloves, crushed
Sprinkling of sea salt
Olive oil (preferably El Ouazzania)
2 lemons
Optional: 2 or 3 red chilli peppers, two tablespoons of
    honey, icing sugar

First, you (or your butcher) need to spatchcock the chicken: this involves removing the spine with a heavy knife in order to open up the bird. Insert the knife at the neck end, pass it through the length of the bird and then apply your weight to it to cut right though one side of the backbone; then repeat the exercise on the other side. (If you have a pair of kitchen shears, so much the better. Place the chicken breast-side down, cut round the backbone and remove it.) Keep the backbone and make a quick chicken stock using it.

Now comes the fun bit. Trim all the excess fatty skin of the bird and lay it down flat with the breast facing towards you. Take a sharp knife and cut deep slashes into the flesh all the way across from the legs, through the breast and to the other side. Now shake generous of quantities of *ras el-hanout* over it, rubbing it all over both sides of the bird, and making sure you massage deep into the incisions you've made with the knife. Spoon at least six tablespoons of olive oil and two of fresh lemon juice over the top, then turn the bird several times in this marinade. Place in a bowl, breast facing up, and cover with the garlic and sea salt. Leave in the fridge for a least a couple of hours.

When ready to cook, place under the grill in a roasting tray and grill on each side for ten minutes, taking care not to let it burn. Turn off the grill and change to the oven setting, at around 180 degrees, and finish off by roasting. Depending on the size of the bird, it should take about another fifteen to twenty minutes. Once the juices run clear, it's cooked.

Now, how to serve it? You could of course eat it as it is, but another method – shocking but delicious – is to turn the grill back on, sprinkle the bird with icing sugar and brown that a little under the grill. Alternatively, you could chop and seed your red chillis, sprinkle them on top of the bird with a couple of spoonfuls of honey and, again, cook a little more under the grill. I find the combination of honey, chilli and sea salt irresistible – even if it isn't Moroccan.

The bird will have thrown off some roasting juices: get rid of the excess fat, and combine the juices with a little reduced chicken stock (made using the backbone of the chicken, should you have done that), allow to reduce further until syrupy, and serve on the side. To accompany this sumptuous dish, you could serve rice, couscous, saffron potatoes or garlic spinach, plus a few wedges of lemon.

MAIN COURSES: FISH

We don't eat enough fish in this country, and Irish recipes for it are invariably basic and heavy, often with no respect for the fish – based on our fear of not getting enough to eat and being left still hungry. We need to rethink our approach to fish and indeed our approach to eating – in these times, it would be good to eat less and throw away less. A trip to the supermarket often results in overbuying, with the result that 20 percent of purchases end up in the bin. Only buy what you need.

This next recipe is a result of my travels in Spain, where I discovered this delicious dish in the town of Jerez de la Frontera. It can be a tapa, a small main course or a big main course – the choice is yours. In the recipe, the tuna is more cooked than we here in Ireland are used to, so if that offends your sensitive post-Tiger palate or is too expensive for your post-Tiger wallet, substitute for a cheaper, less noble fish or use your loaf – gastro-pun intended – and just cook it less. In any case, the *encebollado* sauce ('having been onioned') keeps it all deliciously moist. The other expensive item, sherry vinegar, we already have.

Atún encebollado

One chunk of fresh tuna per person
2 cloves of garlic
2 onions
1 glass of dry sherry or 1 glass of white wine and a
*   little sherry vinegar*
Salt and pepper
Fresh oregano, chopped
Spanish olive oil
1 bay leaf
A little parsley

Heat the olive oil in a large pan and then add the onions, sliced into thin rounds, plus the chopped garlic and the bay leaf.

Allow to cook until soft and translucent. Now add the tuna in chunks or cubes, together with the sherry (or the wine and sherry vinegar). Season with a little salt and pepper and add the chopped parsley and oregano.

Cover with a lid and allow to cook at a simmer. The tuna is ready when it's cooked all the way through, as per the local tradition, but as I have said, you can simply cook it a little less, if you like your tuna rare.

Another fish dish I came across in Spain that I liked a lot was this next one, whose sauce came from the town of Rota near Jerez and was thus named *a la roteña*. Again, it could be served as a tapa, a *media ración* (half-portion) or *ración* (full portion).

Baked fish a la roteña

4 fillets of firm white fish such as cod, hake,
*   gurnard or even ling*
1 kg ripe tomatoes
1 onion
350g green peppers
500g baby potatoes
2 cloves of garlic
Glass of dry sherry
Bunch of parsley
Olive oil
Salt and pepper

Make a cross in the base of the tomatoes, plunge them into boiling water for thirteen seconds, remove, refresh and then peel them.

Thinly slice the garlic as well as the onion and fry these together with the green peppers, sliced into julienne, without browning them. After a few minutes, add the tomatoes, together with the parsley and seasoning, and leave to simmer.

In another pan, sear the fish on both sides in a little oil, then pour the sherry on top. Cover the fish with the sauce, leave on the heat for one minute, then transfer to an oven pre-heated to 180 degrees for around five minutes.

Pre-cook the potatoes, slice and place in the bottom of each serving dish. Serve the fish on top with plenty of sauce.

Grilled hake with leek and ginger sauce

Now, you want simple? You got simple.

Olive oil
5 or 6 leeks
1 small piece of fresh ginger
Salt and pepper
Zest and juice of 1 lemon
4 fillets of hake

Wash the leeks thoroughly, trim, and slice the whites thinly.

Peel the ginger and chop it finely.

Heat the oil in a pan and fry the leeks and ginger together for around five minutes without browning.

After this time, when the leeks have 'melted', stir in all the lemon juice and its zest and season with sea salt and fresh black pepper.

Grill or fry the hake and serve with the sauce. (It will go equally well with many other fish.)

Three ways with mackerel

I love cooking and eating mackerel – indeed, you could use mackerel in the tuna recipe above, if your budget does not allow for the latter. As I mentioned in the introduction, I remember a Tuesday in France many years ago where the local fishmonger would come round the village in a van and sell his wares directly – a practice probably now banned by evil bureaucrats. There we bought a huge mackerel, which was then cooked in the following manner and plonked on the table, to be attacked and eaten, and washed down with lashings of local white plonk. Unfortunately, we rarely see huge mackerel in this country, but here's the same simple recipe for a smaller one.

Whole baked mackerel with white wine, garlic and pearl onions

1 medium-sized mackerel per person
150g baby onions
1 glass dry white wine, such as Muscadet
1 clove of garlic
50g butter
1 lemon (for garnish)
Squeeze of lemon juice
1 bunch of parsley
1 bay leaf

Have the fishmonger clean the mackerel and remove the head and tail if desired.

Peel the onions but leave them whole.

Crush the garlic and chop it finely.

Place the mackerel, baby onions and garlic in an oven dish. Add a few knobs of butter, season well with sea salt and black pepper and then pour the wine over the fish. Add more wine, to bring it halfway up the body of the fish, if necessary. Add the bay leaves and place in an oven preheated to 180 degrees.

When the fish is almost ready, remove from the oven and turn the fish. Scatter finely chopped parsley into the sauce and add a squeeze of lemon juice. Return to the oven for another few minutes. A medium-sized fish should take around fifteen to twenty minutes.

Serve piping hot, with buttered rice or potatoes. Garnish with lemon wedges.

Grilled mackerel fillets with chermoula and stuffed prunes

This is altogether more exotic, and a good way to introduce *chermoula*, one of my favourite North African sauces for fish, and one which should gain wider currency. We'll be returning to it again in a few recipes' time, because it is an easy yet delicious sauce that can accompany may different fish. Quite apart from the sauce, the combination of the stuffed prunes and the mackerel is utterly delicious.

2 medium mackerel fillets per person
3 prunes per serving
Blanched toasted almonds
2 cloves of garlic
Flat-leaf parsley
Fresh coriander
Paprika
Cumin
Cayenne pepper
Lemon juice
Olive oil
A little water

Make the *chermoula* either by pounding the garlic in a mortar and pestle or by pulsing it in a food processor. Add generous handfuls of parsley and coriander plus two teaspoons each of paprika and cumin, one of cayenne pepper and a tablespoon of lemon juice. Mix this to a paste and then add a few tablespoons of olive oil, plus a little water if necessary.

Take some of the *chermoula*, rub it all over both sides of the fish and leave to marinate for about twenty minutes. Then grill the fish, allowing roughly five minutes per side.

During this time, toast the whole blanched almonds. Then make an incision in each prune and push an almond into it.

Serve the mackerel with the prunes and a little *chermoula* drizzled around the fish. Serve with parsleyed baby potatoes, rice or couscous.

Pan-fried mackerel with tomato and corn salsa and potato salad

This one is a quick and easy way to prepare mackerel for an informal supper. Invariably, the tinned tomatoes will come from Italy and should be quite tasty. You could buy the chopped ones instead or you could buy the tins that come with herbs already in them, for an even tastier result.

1 mackerel per person
1 packet of baby corn
Olive oil
Salt and pepper
1 tin of plum tomatoes
1 red onion
Fresh coriander
Lime juice
Lemon juice
1 large red chilli
1 small bag of baby potatoes
1 head of garlic
Flat-leaf parsley
Cider vinegar

To make the salsa, grill the baby corn all over until it's coloured and then chop up into small pieces. Combine this with the tinned tomatoes (chop them up if they're whole), the red onion, finely chopped, one tablespoon each of lime and lemon juice, salt and pepper, the chilli, chopped, and plenty of fresh coriander.

Boil the potatoes and, while they're still hot, cut them in half and dress with a sauce made from three parts oil to one part vinegar, plus the garlic and parsley, both roughly chopped.

Pan-fry each seasoned mackerel in a little olive oil.

When ready, place the potato salad in a pastry ring and mould it. Place the cooked mackerel on top and spoon the salsa over and around. Garnish with sprigs of fresh coriander and wedges of lemon.

Three ways with mussels

Preparing and cooking mussels is a lot of fun – even more fun is going and gathering them yourself, which is how I was introduced to them for the first time at seventeen years of age. People tend to baulk at the notion of cooking them, though, and the mollusc is largely misunderstood. There isn't really that much preparation, it just takes a little time; if you can recruit some helping pairs of hands, the work goes quickly. There are several ways you can approach them – one way is to clean them by running cold water over the shells and removing the 'beards' as you go along. If there are excessive amounts of shellfish stuck to the shell, you can knock these off with the blade of a knife. Some people say that you should leave the mussels in cold water that contains flour – the mussel thinks that the flour is food, opens up and releases any impurities that may be contained within its shell. In either case, the most important thing is to discard any which are open and which do not immediately close again following a sharp blow to the shell. The cooking itself is simple – at its most basic, you only need a little water, onions, butter and parsley. I stress *a little* water; this must not cover the mussel, because it is the steam from this which kills the shellfish and causes it to release its juices, making the sauce. If there is too much water covering the ones on the bottom, the mussel will not open. Here are a couple of recipes to whet your appetite.

Mussels marinière

3 litres of mussels
A glass of dry white wine, such as Muscadet or
*   Gros Plant*
Large bunch of parsley
2 chopped onions
1 crushed clove of garlic (optional)
100g butter

This is one of the classic recipes for mussels – and one of the least understood. There is no cream, nor any need for it. It can be kept as cheap as you like, even eschewing wine, though the latter undoubtedly helps. The onions can be replaced with shallots if your budget will stretch to that.

Begin by cleaning the mussels, removing their beards and discarding any that are open. In a very large pot (you've got one, right?), place a very small quantity of water on the bottom, just enough to make steam, and then place the mussels on top. Turn up the heat and cover with the lid. After about five minutes, when the mussels start to open, add the chopped onion, the chopped parsley, the garlic, if desired, and then the wine.

Turn the heat down, toss the mussels a little and cover with the lid once more. They will be ready in a few minutes, when the shells are wide open; there is nothing to be gained from any further cooking. Serve immediately with crusty bread or, if you're Belgian or have been to Bruges, chips.

Gratin of curried mussels with spinach

The following recipe is one of the many ways in which mussels can be prepared and served. I like eating them from their shells but I also wanted to give a different recipe where the mussels are actually removed and gratinéed, for a fancier dinner. In the first instance, the mussels can be cooked as per the first part of the preceding recipe – the trick is not to overcook them, as they are going to be heated again.

1kg cleaned and cooked mussels, removed from their shells (reserve the cooking liquid)
250g cooked spinach
Small tub of double cream
1 teaspoon of curry powder, turmeric and garam masala

Warm the cooking liquid from the mussels in a pot and add the spices. Allow these to cook slowly for a few minutes before bringing to the boil. Add a little cream and leave to simmer. Correct the seasoning. While you're doing this, remove all the mussels from their shells.

Quickly blanch the spinach in lightly salted,

boiling water, refresh and then drain off all the excess water.

Now press the spinach down in an oven dish and arrange the mussels over this. Pour the sauce all over the mussels, covering them. Place under a grill in the oven and gratiné them for about five minutes, or until the mixture browns. Serve immediately.

Spaghettini with mussels and cherry tomatoes

Now a hearty use of mussels in a pasta dish; the idea is not dissimilar to the classic *spaghetti alle vongole* – just a little more involved. Besides, you can't count on finding clams or vongole on a daily basis. This is great fun for a supper dish with friends. You can use spaghetti for this recipe but I'll insist on my beloved *spaghettini*.

> *450g spaghettini (well, we're hungry!)*
> *1.5 litres mussels*
> *3 cloves of garlic*
> *1 tub of cherry tomatoes*
> *A little sugar*
> *Glass of dry white wine*
> *Sea salt and black pepper*
> *A few leaves of basil or a small bunch of parsley*
> *A small jar of capers*

Begin by cleaning the mussels.

Have two pots standing by – one to cook the pasta and the other to make the sauce. In one, cook your crushed, chopped garlic in a little olive oil before adding the cherry tomatoes, which have been cut in half. Leave this to cook for a couple of minutes over a low heat before adding the wine, the capers, a pinch of sugar and finally the mussels themselves. Cover with a lid and allow to cook.

Meanwhile, boil plenty of water in the other pot and cook the pasta until it's al dente. Drain, but reserve a little of the cooking liquid to keep the pasta hot. A nice manner of presentation would be to transfer the pasta to a large serving dish and then pour all the tomato and mussel mix on top. To serve, tear a few basil leaves over it or sprinkle with chopped parsley.

Baked whole fish with chermoula and couscous

Now here's our *chermoula* again. This time it's part-nered with a whole fish, something I love to eat. Try and get something like a gurnard, which is chunky and relatively cheap. You can serve it with rice or potatoes, but why not try this simple way of preparing a side dish of couscous?

1 whole fish (such as gurnard), gutted
Bay leaves
Salt and pepper
Coarse sea salt
Cinnamon
1 packet of couscous
1 large bouquet of coriander
Salt
4 cloves of garlic
Water
1 teaspoon of chopped red chilli
1 red pepper, seeded and chopped
1 tablespoon cumin
2 tablespoons fresh lemon juice
Olive oil

First, rub the fish all over with olive oil, salt and pepper: do this to the inside too, and place bay leaves inside. Roast in a medium hot oven for about twenty minutes, or until it is completely cooked.

Make the *chermoula* by chopping the coriander and then crushing it with the garlic cloves and salt; transfer to a blender and pulse with the other ingredients, and around three to four tablespoons of olive oil to bind.

Moisten the couscous with water, allow to expand, then warm in a pan over a low heat. When the water is fully absorbed, place in an oven for a few minutes to complete the cooking. Season with fresh coriander, salt, cinnamon and a few knobs of butter or olive oil.

When the fish is ready, serve at once with the *chermoula* over and around it and the couscous on the side.

Ray wings with lemon and caper butter

I know that bony fish scare a lot of people, and so I imagine they are particularly put off by the thought of dealing with ray, though it's an easy enough fish to cook and one of the most delicious. Here is a very easy recipe for it; the only vaguely tricky part is clarifying the butter. You will need a steamer. You can use a steam basket or you can pick up one of those Thai bamboo steamers for very little outlay.

4 ray wings (also known as skate)
100g butter
2 lemons
50g tiny capers
Salt and black pepper
Baby potatoes

Cook the ray in a steamer for twenty minutes: if you're using the bamboo steamer, check that the water does not evaporate below it. When the fish is cooked, remove the skin (it should come away quite easily) and, using your fingers, all the bones.

Meanwhile (not forgetting that water), clarify the butter by gently warming it in a saucepan and allowing it to melt. A foam will rise to the top; skim that off, and you're left with clarified butter.

All there is to do now is plate the ray and spoon the clarified butter over it. Season with salt and pepper, and sprinkle with capers and a quick twist of lemon juice. Magic. Oh – and the potatoes, simply boil.

VEGETABLES AND FUNNY LITTLE THINGS ON THE SIDE

Patatas a la sierra

Let's start off with potatoes. The thing which I found odd when in Spain for the first time a couple of years ago was the number of dishes that contained potatoes, whereas I had envisaged a potato-free zone for the duration. They're everywhere! In fact, one night I decided to have a tapa of sausages which sounded rather appetizing: to accompany it, I chose potatoes in garlic, imagining them to be sautéed with garlic. Not so – they turned out to be a huge dish of garlic potato salad, enough for four! As for the sausages, I gave up counting them at twenty, and they came on a large bed of fried potatoes. The whole lot cost €6. The Spanish have it right, and it is with pleasure that I note that the *taperías* are the beneficiaries of the downturn over there (whereas here we flock to the fast-food joints).

Anyway, the reason I'm telling you all this is that one *tapería* offered, among other things, a 'potato list' of the various ways in which it served the humble tuber. Eschewing the ubiquitous *patatas bravas*, I plumped for these, the *patatas a la sierra*, which had a romantic ring to them, given that '*sierra*' means mountains, giving me fanciful notions of a shared potato-fest for two, on top of a balmy Spanish hilltop. They turned out to be delicious albeit in a distinctly non-amorous sort of way, and this is my take on them.

In fact, they are so good, you might need to double up the parsimonious quantities given here.

1 large potato per person
1 white onion
Diced Iberian ham or smoked lardons
Pinch of smoked paprika or, if you have or can get it, pimentón
1 clove of garlic
Coarse sea salt and black pepper
4 oyster mushrooms per person
Olive oil

Peel the potatoes, slice them into rounds, then fry them gently in a little olive oil. When they begin to soften and colour, add the onion, sliced into rings, and the garlic, crushed and roughly chopped. Follow this with the cubes of ham or, failing that, some smoked lardons or pancetta. When everything is almost cooked, add the oyster mushrooms (whole) and allow them to cook in the heat of the potatoes. Season with paprika (or *pimentón*), black pepper and sea salt. Serve immediately.

Potatoes baked with yoghurt and Cashel Blue

Here's a dead simple Irish potato dish that would make an excellent supper for anyone, vegetarian or not. The cream in it is nice but not strictly necessary. This dish goes well with a crisp green salad and one of the vinaigrettes at the beginning of the book. A glass of wine would not be out of place either.

4 large potatoes
Large tub of plain yoghurt
100g pouring cream
100g Cashel Blue
Salt and pepper

Begin by cooking the potatoes in their skins in boiling water; remove from the water well before they are fully cooked. Drain and refresh.

When they are cold, make a hole in the upper part of each one, removing a good third of the potato. Break this part up with a fork and mix it with the yoghurt, the cream and the cheese. Season well.

Spoon the mixture into the hole you have made, and fill it, then place in a preheated oven (180 degrees) and leave for thirty minutes.

Mashed potato

Mashed potato is one of my favourite things – isn't it everybody's? With a little care, it can be perfect; it can be eaten just as it is or used as a garnish for sausages, roasts or as a topping for the likes of shepherd's pie.

1 kg good firm potatoes (like Roosters)
A pinch of salt
1 bay leaf
2 tablespoons of olive oil
150ml milk
Sea salt (to season)
Ground white pepper
Freshly grated nutmeg

Making mashed potato need not involve peeling the potatoes, boiling them and waiting until they're fully cooked – which often puts people off because of the time it takes. You can gain time by cutting the potatoes into smaller pieces after peeling. Then plunge them into cold, salted water, together with the bay leaf, and bring to the boil. Lower the heat and leave to simmer. They should be ready to mash in a quarter of an hour. Test one piece with a knife and drain.

Return them to the saucepan to mash: off the heat, mash them thoroughly before adding the butter a little at a time, and all the olive oil. Combine these ingredients with a wooden spoon, adding the milk, which you have heated, until a soft, smooth mash is obtained. Finally, season to taste with the salt, pepper and nutmeg.

Sautéed potatoes

A short time ago, I absent-mindedly made some sautéed potatoes for my young son, who afterwards declared them 'the best I've ever eaten in my life'. This caused me to sit up and decide that I'd better make a note as to how I did them, for in sooth, it was really using all that I had to hand on the day, to avoid leaving the house in the pouring rain for further ingredients. It struck me then that they were an ideal candidate for this book, given that I'd innocently made something rather good out of very little.

It's important to stress that this isn't the classic recipe for sautéed potatoes, just what I happened to make on the day. Sorry to be so vague, but I can't even remember what they were served with. They would suit roast chicken, steak, sausages – anything like that.

A couple of large potatoes per person, or about four Charlotte potatoes each, sliced not too thinly. (I prefer to leave the skins on.)

1 onion
1 clove of garlic
A few rashers of bacon
A small bunch of parsley

Salt and pepper
80g butter
A little olive oil

Melt the butter and the olive oil in a pan and, when it's foaming, add the potatoes. Keep the heat at medium and sauté the potatoes frequently until they begin to colour. At that point, add the thinly sliced onions, followed by the rashers, which have been cut up small like lardons, and then the garlic. Continue to sauté over a low flame. Finally, season with salt and pepper and add the parsley.

Now that I think about it, these are very like a *sarladaise* potato (a French method of sautéing potatoes in goose fat with bacon lardons). You could call it that if you like and are seeking to impress with your wide knowledge of regional French potato recipes.

Albondigas

Here's yet another popular Spanish tapa: *albondigas*, or meatballs.

1 green pepper
Olive oil
400g minced beef or steak
200g minced pork
Breadcrumbs
Salt and pepper
Nutmeg
Chopped parsley
2 cloves of garlic
1 tin of plum tomatoes
Dried oregano
100g flaked almonds

Chop both the pepper and the onion finely and cook them over a low heat in a tablespoon of olive oil until soft, then leave to cool.

In a large bowl, mix with the meats, breadcrumbs, salt, nutmeg and parsley. Then fashion this mixture into small meatballs and cook them all over in some hot oil for about five minutes; then leave to rest.

Chop up the garlic and cook it in oil over a low heat for a few minutes. Add the tomatoes and their juice and break up with a wooden spoon. Sprinkle with oregano and adjust the seasoning. Add the meatballs and leave them to simmer in the sauce for around twenty minutes.

Transfer to plates and sprinkle with toasted flaked almonds.

Stir-fried broccoli with cashew nuts, garlic and oyster sauce

Broccoli? I love it. Shall I count the ways? Here's one.

Groundnut oil
Oyster sauce
2 heads of broccoli
2 cloves of garlic
100g cashew nuts

Heat a tablespoon of oil in a wok or pan and fry the cashew nuts until golden. Remove the nuts from the pan but leave the oil.

Cut the broccoli into florets, add these to the oil and stir-fry for a couple of minutes. Crush and chop the garlic and add this too.

Then add a little water, turn up the heat and allow to boil, to finish cooking the broccoli.

When the broccoli is just cooked, add about three tablespoons of oyster sauce and stir in. Return the cashew nuts to the mixture and serve.

Broccoli with anchovy and garlic

And here's another.

2 heads of broccoli
2 cloves of garlic
1 tin of anchovies
60ml olive oil

This borrows from the tradition of the *bagna cauda* dip in the Piedmont region in northern Italy, where the new vegetables are celebrated by being given a hot bath.

Cook your broccoli in boiling salted water for a few minutes, then drain. Meanwhile, place the anchovies in the olive oil over a medium heat and let them melt. Crush and chop the garlic, throw this into the oil and allow to cook for a few minutes, then whisk the lot together. Spoon the anchovy sauce over the hot broccoli. If you have some pine kernels lying around, they wouldn't go amiss either.

Spinach salad with chickpeas and artichokes

I love anything involving spinach and I especially enjoy it when it's raw: the flavour and texture are incomparable. Combined with such earthy ingredients as chickpeas and artichokes, it makes for an intensely satisfying salad. Note that artichoke hearts can be bought already grilled, but you can do them yourself and save a few euro. If you're bringing these ingredients with you for a simple and healthy lunch, the vinaigrette should be made separately and only added at the last minute, as otherwise the spinach would be 'overcooked' by the vinegar.

1 tin of organic chickpeas, drained
1 jar of artichoke hearts
250g young spinach leaves
4 portobello mushrooms
Fresh parsley
Wedge of pecorino cheese
Red wine vinegar
Dijon mustard
Groundnut oil

Begin by grilling the artichoke hearts gently until they are just coloured, and at the same time heat the chickpeas gently with a little oil. Place the mushrooms (seasoned and lightly oiled) under a grill and cook for around five minutes.

Make a vinaigrette by combining three parts oil to one part vinegar. Mix the oil and mustard together first (a good dollop) and then add the vinegar. Season with salt and ground black pepper.

Place the spinach leaves in a bowl and lightly salt them. Toss them with the vinaigrette (this will cook them a little) and then add the mushrooms (quartered), the warm chickpeas and the artichoke hearts. Toss well.

Arrange on a serving plate with parsley and shavings of fresh pecorino on top.

For a more hearty supper dish, you could add grilled pancetta or bacon lardons. Grilled asapargus would be excellent in this salad too.

Three simple Moroccan salads

I love the fresh and unusual salads of Morocco, so here are three of them that could be eaten before, or with, some of the dishes from that country that I've included in the book.

Orange and date salad

6 sweet clementines
Handful of mint leaves
Box of Medjool dates
1 tablespoon orange-flower water
90g almonds

Peel the oranges and trim of all the membrane, exposing the flesh. Cut into segments between the membranes, holding over a bowl to catch any juices.

Place all the oranges in the bowl together with the juice and add the orange-flower water; leave to chill in the fridge for a short while.

Serve on a wide plate with the dates sliced lengthwise and scattered with the almonds, which you will have toasted first. Shred the mint leaves and spread them on top.

Orange and carrot salad

6 clementines
2 tablespoons lemon juice
500g carrots
2 teaspoons cinnamon
1 tablespoon caster sugar
1 tablespoon orange-flower water
Mint leaves

Prepare the clementines as in the recipe above.

Clean the carrots and cut into julienne or grate them coarsely. Add the cinnamon, some sugar, a little salt and the orange-flower water. Combine all the ingredients and leave to chill. Serve with shredded mint leaves.

Orange and radish salad

6 clementines
12 radishes
1 tablespoon lemon juice
2 tablespoons caster sugar
2 tablespoons olive oil
1 tablespoon orange-flower water
Ground cinnamon
Mint leaves

Prepare the clementines as in the first recipe but drain the juice and keep to one side.

Wash and trim the radishes, then slice them very thinly. Add to the bowl with the oranges.

In a smaller bowl, mix the orange juice with the lemon juice, sugar, olive oil and a pinch of salt. Mix this and pour over the radishes and oranges before sprinkling with the orange-flower water. Chill before serving and sprinkle with cinnamon and shredded mint leaves.

Tempura of vegetables

Once you realise that tempura is extremely easy and cost-effective to do – and not some kind of mysterious, impenetrable Asian method of cooking – you'll probably be doing it on a nightly basis, and soon be using chopsticks to remove the vegetables from the hot oil. It's fun and it's convivial. There are a few things to bear in mind, however. First, make sure that the water you use is ice-cold. This keeps the oil at bay during the cooking and results in the light batter of properly made tempura. You could even have a few ice cubes standing by to make sure the batter stays cold. To further refine the batter, you could also use sparkling mineral water instead of tap water. In addition – oh happy day – you're not to worry about lumps, nor are you to overbeat the batter. In fact, you don't even need to let it stand. Apart from the batter, you need to heat the oil to 190 degrees. And remember, hot oil is potentially dangerous, so approach with care.

100g plain flour plus 1 tablespoon cornflour
Pinch of fine sea salt
200ml ice-cold water or sparkling mineral water
Ice cubes on standby

Vegetables – choose from carrot, turnip, cauliflower, red pepper, aubergines, courgettes and mushrooms (preferably shiitake)

When the oil is hot, make the batter. Mix the flour and the cornflour with the salt and then add the water. Quickly whisk it to combine the ingredients and form a dough, but don't overbeat it and, as I said, don't worry about lumps. There. That's it. Ready.

Slice up all the vegetables, not too thickly. Dip the vegetables quickly into the batter and then into the oil, using chopsticks, if you're adept. When crispy and fried golden, remove and place on some kitchen roll to absorb any excess fat. Don't place too many items in the oil at one time, as this lowers the temperature.

For a simple dipping sauce to accompany it, combine three tablespoons of soy sauce, three tablespoons of dry sherry, one tablespoon of sugar, and the zest of one lemon.

Pastas, Omelettes and Quick Dishes and Snacks

Here are several pasta dishes that have always appealed to me. They use what I have always believed to be the correct pasta pertinent to the dish – for example, we will often see spaghetti partnered with the classic carbonara, but using a hollow pasta means that the sauce goes inside the pasta as well as outside, providing a more natural creamy finish. Similarly, the correct pasta in the city of Bologna (better known nationally as *Bologna la grassa* – referring to its rich,hearty and, let's face it, fattening recipes) for the eponymous bolognese sauce is tagliatelle and not spaghetti. When in Rome, don't you know . . .

According to my book of Judaeo-Italian recipes from the Lazio-Rome area, there is no room for cream in carbonara, and I prefer leaving it out. It's included here in the recipe should you wish to add it, but the coal-burners of the region had no money to be spending on such luxuries.

Crème fraiche may be replaced by cream, and pancetta by bacon.

Maccheroni alla carbonara

200g diced pancetta
Olive oil
250g short maccheroni
6 egg yolks
150g Parmesan cheese
1 small tub crème fraiche (optional)
Salt and black pepper

Begin by frying the diced pancetta in a little oil over a low heat until it crispens.

Meanwhile, beat all the yolks as though for an omelette, and then season. Then add a generous tablespoon of crème fraiche (this can be omitted if preferred) and half the Parmesan, grated. Whisk well.

Throw the maccheroni into a large pot of boiling salted water and cook to just under al dente, then drain, retaining a little of the cooking water. Add the pasta immediately to the pancetta and oil and toss, before removing the pan from the heat. Now add the egg and Parmesan and mix in order to coat each piece of pasta.

Serve straightaway, with extra Parmesan.

Paglia e fieno con piselli

This has long been a personal favourite: the yellow and green fettucine used in the dish look great but are also the reason for the title of the dish, *paglia e fieno* or 'hay and straw'. Again, this recipe contains cream but, given the flavours of the ham, peas and white wine, I believe it could easily be left out, should you prefer, or in the interests of cutting back. Throwing a little Parmesan into the sauce (as well as liberally sprinkling it on top when the dish is ready) will in itself render the sauce 'creamy'.

125g yellow fettucine
125g green fettucine
1 small tub of cream or crème fraiche
60g butter
1 tin of young peas (or 1 packet of frozen petits pois)
1 slice of Parma ham per person, shredded
Salt and pepper
Glass of dry white wine
2 shallots
120g Parmesan cheese

Chop the shallots finely and cook them in the pan in a little butter until soft. Now add the peas and a little white wine. When the peas are warmed through and the wine has reduced, add the cream, followed by the ham.

Meanwhile, cook the pasta (all together) until almost al dente, then drain, reserving a little of the cooking liquid.

Grate the cheese and mix half of it in the sauce; arrange the pasta on a serving plate and spoon the sauce around it. Finish off with a little more cheese and serve immediately.

Tagliatelle alla bolognese

This is a fairly accurate recipe for bolognese sauce. You could make it in quantity and use it when needed for this recipe, or cheat and turn the same sauce into a shepherd's pie, or use it in stuffed tomatoes or even a moussaka, adding a few aubergines, potatoes and mint. Note that this recipe uses three different kinds of meat (which of itself is correct but does not include the requisite minced veal of Bologna; no matter, it will still be delicious). Minced venison is becoming more popular these days; it is healthy, lean and nutritious, so you could easily substitute that for, say, the minced beef. Most of the ingredients in this recipe are cheap, such as the pasta and the vegetables, but you may baulk at the number of ingredients used.

Fear not! You can of course cut out many of these ingredients: I looked at the recipe given in a cookery book aimed at impecunious students and they left out both the Parma ham and the chicken livers, while substituting vegetable oil for olive and bacon for pancetta. Clearly, many of my ingredients (such as the porcini mushrooms) can take a hike, but I would urge you to try the full recipe a least once.

Olive oil
Unsalted butter
Small packet of pancetta
2 slices of Parma ham
1 packet of dried porcini mushrooms
1 onion
2 cloves of garlic
1 carrot
1 stick of celery
1 bunch of parsley
1 tin chopped tomatoes
1 bottle red wine
100g minced beef
100g minced pork
100g minced chicken or turkey
50g chicken livers
Salt and black pepper
Nutmeg
200g Parmesan cheese

Melt the butter in a little olive oil and cook the pancetta and the Parma ham together for around ten minutes. Now add the onion, diced carrot and sliced celery, and cook for another ten minutes. Soak the porcini mushrooms in warm water, then remove and chop, reserving the liquid. Add these too, stirring constantly.

Now add all the meats, including the chicken livers, and brown for around ten minutes.

After this time, add a generous glass of red wine, as well as the tinned tomatoes. Strain the mushroom liquid and add this too. Season with salt, pepper and nutmeg and leave to simmer.

Cook the tagliatelle until just under al dente; drain, keeping some of the cooking liquid. Arrange in a serving plate and spoon the sauce over the pasta generously. Serve with heaps of grated Parmesan cheese.

Spaghetti with lemon and basil

Here's a very different pasta dish from the ones we usually see on the menus of Italian restaurants – but no less delicious for that. You can put it together in no time, and you may already have many of the ingredients to hand, with the exception of the basil. (At a push, you could use parsley instead.)

Packet of spaghetti or spaghettini
Bunch of fresh basil
4 lemons
Salt and black pepper
Olive oil
Parmesan cheese

Juice all the lemons and whisk the juice with around 150ml of olive oil. Then add the grated Parmesan – enough to make the emulsion thick. Now season it with salt and black pepper.

Then cook the spaghetti. Drain and return to the saucepan with a little of the cooking water.

Add the sauce to the pasta in the saucepan and mix it in well; at the last minute, stir in all the chopped basil.

Stuffed tomatoes

This is a great recipe for a fun snack or supper dish. Use beef tomatoes, as they will hold quite a lot of the filling.

1 or 2 beef tomatoes per person (depending on how big the tomatoes are – and how hungry you are)
1 onion
1 clove of garlic
About 100g of minced beef per person
Dried herbes de Provence
1 tin of chopped tomatoes
Salt and black pepper
Teaspoon of sugar
Easy-cook rice
Glass of white wine

Slice along the top of each tomato, reserve this 'lid' and scoop out the insides, saving them for later.

Dice the onion, crush the garlic and fry them together in a little oil. Then add the minced beef and continue to fry until brown all over. Add the chopped tomatoes, season well and allow to cook. When ready, spoon into the tomatoes' cavities and fill.

Take the scooped-out insides of the tomatoes and chop them well. Transfer to an oven dish, season with salt and pepper, and add the teaspoon of sugar, a generous pinch of herbes de Provence and the white wine. Put each tomato on top of this mixture and then place in an oven, preheated to around 190 degrees, for about thirty minutes. Keep an eye on them from time to time and reduce the heat if necessary: you want the flesh of the tomatoes to cook but not to become so mushy that they split.

While they're roasting, cook the rice, drain and season. Add a splash of olive oil or a small knob of butter and serve with the tomatoes and the impromptu sauce.

Don't forget that if you've made and frozen the Bolognese sauce from that recipe, it could be used to stuff these tomatoes.

Shepherd's pie (hachis Parmentier)

As an impressionable young lad, I was privileged to have Saturday lunch in a French household and, having stayed the night before, took part in the actual preparations for the lunch. The main dish that day was called *hachis Parmentier*, which we know as shepherd's or cottage pie – but the distinctions in those two appellations do not exist in the original French version, which is the daddy of them all when it comes to leftovers. That morning, I watched spellbound as the 'man of the house' opened a Tupperware thingamajig and began to pass the contents through a massive handheld mincer, which was attached by a clamp to the table. With complete disregard for quantities, he pushed through bits of leftover chicken, fish, steak, roast lamb, fish, huge bunches of parsley and cloves of raw garlic. This all emerged at the other end as an already-appetising-looking mince. Still, I was a bit taken aback, and asked about the fish, at least. He explained to me that this was their lunch every Saturday, composed solely of the previous week's leftovers. Nothing ever went to waste. It was one of the best lunches

I ever had, and I have been making a version of it ever since.

Here is a recipe using the classic ingredients that we know, but do take inspiration from *hachis Parmentier* and incorporate your leftovers. You don't need the big silver antique mixer; just chop up the leftovers uniformly with a sharp knife.

By the way, Auguste Parmentier was the man who introduced the potato to France, and dishes containing potatoes bear his name.

Either 500g of minced beef or 500g of various leftovers, such as roast chicken or pork, sausages especially. (You could also use the bolognese sauce.)
The ingredients for mashed potato, given on page 158
2 onions
2 carrots
2 cloves of garlic
1 bay leaf
Passata or tomato puree
Glass of white wine
Small bunch of parsley, chopped
A little oil
Butter
Small tin of petits pois (optional)

The procedure for this most rustic of dishes is simple enough. However, in order to avoid the finished result being in any way bland, one should take great care to season well and use whatever herbs one has to hand.

Begin by frying the onion, bay leaf and garlic in a frying pan before adding either the raw minced beef or a mixture of some minced beef and plenty of chopped leftovers. Allow to fry and then add the peeled and chopped carrots. When all the meat is browned, add about 50ml of passata or a large tablespoon of tomato puree and stir in, followed by the white wine. Leave to simmer in the pan for about thirty minutes, topping up with a little water if necessary, though the meat should render its own juices. Season with plenty of salt, pepper and nutmeg, and taste to make sure that the seasoning is perfect before transferring to an oven.

While the filling is simmering, make the mash as described in the vegetable chapter.

Preheat the oven to 190 degrees, then transfer the filling to a suitable oven dish and top with the mash. Draw the prongs of a fork along the mash to make lines in it, which will look nice when browned. Place in the oven for at least twenty minutes until the filling is threatening to bubble out and the mash has browned. If the mash hasn't browned at this stage, turn on the grill and brown it that way. A few knobs of butter thrown on top of the mash at this stage will add a touch of luxury.

Finally, note that in France the *hachis* has taken on a new life in restaurants as a confit of duck *hachis*, where all the soft duck flesh is boned and then cooked as a *hachis*. It's not a bad idea at all. If you're over there, watch out for it: *hachis Parmentier de (confit de) canard*.

Huevos revueltos

You sure see a lot of eggs in Spain. No matter what you eat, they are omnipresent: in the mayonnaise that graces the garlic potato salad, or the ubiquitous *ensaladilla russa* (tinned vegetables in mayonnaise from a jar) eaten by Spaniards day or night standing at a bar with a glass of beer, or of course in the tortillas and straightforward egg dishes that appear everywhere. This is one of those dishes, but be advised: '*revueltos*' doesn't mean 'revolting' but something like 'scrambled'. This dish exists just about anywhere Spanish is spoken.

50g good-quality bacon
50g chorizo sausage
4 eggs
Olive oil
2 tablespoons milk
Salt and black pepper

Chop the bacon up small and slice the chorizo (remove the covering first). Fry these two ingredients in a little oil.

Beat the eggs together with the milk, season, then add to the frying pan and whisk together until cooked. They should be light and fluffy.

Other ingredients you could use instead of the bacon and sausage are mushrooms, asparagus, scallions, prawns, Serrano ham and spinach – though not all at once, naturally.

Spinach and Parmesan frittata

Fortunately, I love eggs, so I'm warming to the theme now. While we have the French term 'omelette' in English and are familiar with the word 'tortilla' (which, irritatingly, doesn't always mean 'omelette'), we are less aware of the Italian take on the eggy concoction, referred to as a frittata. Here's one of my favourite Italian frittata recipes, with one of my favourite vegetables, spinach. You'll notice that the Italian frittata is quite similar to the Spanish tortilla, which is up next.

1 bag of spinach
Olive oil
1 onion
1 clove of garlic
9 eggs
Splash of milk
100g Parmesan cheese
Salt and black pepper
2 tomatoes

Blanch the spinach in some boiling salted water; drain, refresh and then chop.

Whisk the eggs (but not too thoroughly) with the milk and grated Parmesan.

Chop the tomatoes and add these to the mix, then season.

Chop the onion and sauté in a pan with a little olive oil for around two minutes, before adding the garlic; cook for another minute. Now add the chopped spinach and spread it all out over the surface of the pan.

Pour the egg mixture over this and allow to set, shaking the pan at the same time. Then either transfer to the oven or place under the grill for another ten to fifteen minutes. (Keep the grill on a low heat so that the frittata cooks and becomes golden brown; don't let it burn.)

A frittata will accomodate a great variety of other ingredients; instead of spinach, you could use sundried tomatoes (cut into very thin strips), chopped black olives, Gorgonzola or even goat's cheese. You could either incorporate these into the frittata or put them on top.

Spanish omelette (aka tortilla de patatas)

The famous Spanish omelette is somewhat sacred in Spain, and it is close to blasphemy to depart from the potato-and-egg-based recipe – as I found to my cost when I once suggested making one with smoked salmon. Horror. Hands thrown up in incredulity.

Immortalised in *Fawlty Towers* when Bernard Cribbins lambasted poor old Basil with his take on the correct ingredients for it, *la tortilla española* can vary greatly in quality within the Iberian peninsula itself but can be truly great in the right establishment.

50ml olive oil
6 medium potatoes
1 onion
6 to 9 eggs
Salt

Those are the ingredients for the tortilla in its most basic form. I have also encountered it with red pepper throughout it – but never with Bernard Cribbins's peas, which he felt were an integral part of the dish. The trick is to cook the sliced potatoes and onion first in plenty of oil with a little salt, without colouring them, and then to drain the oil and place the mixture on some kitchen roll to absorb the excess fat. The oil should be hot enough to cook the vegetables but not so hot that the potatoes burn on the outside and leave the insides raw.

Crack and beat the eggs as for an omelette, and then fold the potatoes and onion into this, and mix well. Heat more oil (but considerably less this time) in a pan over a medium heat and pour the egg mixture in. Spread it out evenly and allow to cook. After a short while, you can examine the underside to see if it has browned; at that point, you're ready to flip it over. Upend the pan onto a large dinner plate so that the tortilla falls out onto it. Return the pan to the heat and, when it's warm once more, slide the tortilla back in, runny side down. Leave to brown on this side for another five minutes and then remove from the heat and allow to settle in the pan.

When ready, slide on to a plate. It can be eaten straightaway while hot, though most authorities will tell you that it requires some time for the flavours to infuse. It can also be eaten cold with crusty bread or cut up into bite-sized pieces as tapas, often with a slice of baguette.

Omelette Parmentière

It's that dude Parmentier again. This popular French omelette is one of my favourites: quick, simple to make, and not requiring as much cooking time as the Spanish and Italian equivalents. Unlike frittata and tortilla, an omelette is often enjoyed *baveuse*, as the French call it – that is to say, runny.

For a single omelette:

3 eggs
2 potatoes, peeled and diced
Salt and black pepper
Chopped parsley
Tablespoon of groundnut oil
Small knob of butter

Heat the oil in a pan and sauté the diced potatoes over a medium heat until cooked and golden. (If you prefer, you could parboil the potatoes first to help them on their way, then finish them off, diced, in the pan, in the manner just described.)

Beat the eggs and season them. If you're going to have the omelette runny, then that's all you need to do to them; otherwise, add a knob of butter to the mixture. Add the chopped parsley.

When the potatoes are cooked, turn the heat up and fold in the eggs. This ensures that the omelette has a lovely appetising golden colour. Then reduce the heat and, using a wooden spatula, keep drawing the eggs toward the centre of the pan, allowing the uncooked egg to run back into the spaces and form an omelette once more. When cooked to your taste, remove from the heat and slide on to a warmed plate, folding one half on top of the other as you go.

Omelettes respond well to all manner of fillings, of course. Mushrooms, herbs, tomatoes and ham are some of the more delicious ingredients, and they don't take long to cook.

Breton galettes

The word *galette* in French is probably as annoying as the word *tortilla* in Spanish for the anglophone world – meaning, as it does, just about anything round.

In Brittany, it is applied to those pancakes (the word is unjust) which are made from dark buckwheat flour and have a savoury filling. It remains my favourite quick meal, something for which I always have the ingredients to hand, and which is essentially dirt-cheap. All you need is the buckwheat flour, tap water and a pinch of salt. It evolved from the Celtic settling of Brittany, where buckwheat grew well. (In fact, it was about the only thing that did, not only thriving in Breton soil but taking a mere forty days to grow.) This recipe shows sheer genius when one considers that nothing else was needed to fashion the actual galettes themselves: no eggs, no cream, no wine, just plain water. And they had *that* in spades – or buckets, I suppose. (Sometimes I wonder about the Celts and what went through their heads: 'Ah, here, I know lads, here's a spiffing wheeze. Let's go live in an area of a country where the terrain is difficult, nothing grows, the food is lousy . . . ' I blame that Vercingetorix.)

Besides that, galettes are good for you, as the

flour that makes them is excellent and has positive benefits on the system. In fact, it is better here in our wee country, where it is not refined as much as in Brittany and is mainly stocked by hippie vegetarian heads in woolly jumpers in health-food shops. Trouble is, it's almost too dark and doesn't look as appetising as the professional item in crêperies throughout Brittany. All my attempts to obtain the same result with a mixture of white and buckwheat flour have come to nought, and so I make it with the hippie flour, since it's only for in-house consumption. In case you think that all this preamble is a bit much for a few lousy galettes, be assured that I intend to share some of the fillings with you too.

For the galettes:

200g buckwheat flour
Half a litre of cold water
Salt

That's it. To make the batter, all you have to do is put the flour in a mixing bowl, make a hole in the centre and start to add the water very slowly, to avoid lumps. Eventually you will achieve a batter that is 'loose' and homogenous but quite thick. If it proves to be too thick, just add more water.

To make a galette, you need a good non-stick pan. (Of course, it would be better if we had all the accoutrements available in Brittany, like a *bilig* (the wooden implement used to spead the batter), to make wafer-thin galettes, but we don't, so let's just deal with it.) Heat said pan quite hot, dip some kitchen roll in plain oil and rub this around the base of the pan (the Bretons use *saindoux*, or lard), wait until it begins to smoke, pour in two ladlefuls of batter – one in the middle and one at the edge – and swivel the pan until they meet. If done properly, the galette will immediately become pockmarked like a lunar landscape and after a minute or so can easily be turned over to cook on the other side.

For the filling:

Far and away the most popular filling for galettes is ham, cheese and an egg – this is known as the *complète*. You crack an egg on the cooked side of the galette, whisk it with a fork as it begins to cook, add the slice of ham and then the grated cheese. When the egg has set, fold the galette over on itself and eat straightaway, with a green salad. Variations include a pure pork sausage (perfect with ice-cold, bone-dry cider), mushrooms, tomatoes, other cheeses. Stuff and nonsense, says I: a Breton galette can't have tomatoes in it; they never heard of them until recently. The *complète* is your only man – and you can leave out the ham if you don't eat flesh.

Crostini

The last decade has seen Italian restaurants throw off their fifties British image and delve into a more authentic Italian cuisine, once they realised that this would please Johnny Anglophone as well. These restaurants have often dredged the depths of regional cuisine for the 'new' Italian specialities, and the *crostino* and *bruschetta* have metamorphosed into sandwiches without a top in the nineties and noughties in this part of the world. Nothing wrong with that per se, except that, at their most basic, they are little more than a peasant snack, often rubbed with little more than garlic and olive oil, to be eaten without ceremony while toiling in the fields. Don't get me wrong, they are both excellent, but it seems to me that they are more apt for our book, and for domestic dining, than for gracing the overpriced tables of fine city-centre restaurants.

4 ripe tomatoes
2 onions
1 clove of garlic
Slices of country bread or baguette, toasted
A little sugar
2 tablespoons of olive oil
Salt and pepper

Easy-peasy. Peel and chop the onions and garlic and fry gently in the olive oil for about ten minutes until cooked.

Then plunge the tomatoes into boiling water for thirteen seconds, having made an incision in the bottom of them: remove and skin them, peel them and chop them up roughly. Add to the onion-and-garlic mixture. Add a little salt, the pinch of sugar and plenty of pepper. Cook for another five minutes and then spoon onto the grilled bread.

Alternatively, you could just peel the tomatoes, chop them up and mix with olive oil, chopped basil and salt. Leave for about an hour and then spread onto the crostini. Deliciously simple.

As for *bruschetta*, more often than not it's just a larger slice of bread, toasted with olive oil and rubbed with garlic. You could put the same toppings on them as for the *crostini* above, but the larger playing field allows for a little more imagination. Incidentally, calling into the more popular supermarkets in the country in the early evening often means that you can pick up ciabatta and other breads at knock-down prices as they try to clear their shelves.

Chargrilled mixed peppers with basil, anchovy and capers, served with garlic bruschetta

This is at once a colourful and delicious simple lunch dish – full of traditional Italian flavours. Do try to buy the best anchovies you can afford, as this will make all the difference.

Twelve peppers, six red and six yellow
1 loaf of country Italian bread such as pugliese or
*   ciabatta*
Extra-virgin olive oil
Black pepper and sea salt
3 cloves of garlic
1 bunch of fresh basil
50g capers
120g good-quality marinated anchovies

Begin by grilling the peppers all over until blackened: to remove the skins, place all of these into a plastic bag and seal it. Leave until they have cooled.

When cool enough, rub the peppers with your hands and the skin will come off; rinse under cold water to remove the seeds.

Place all the peppers on a large platter and arrange over them thin slices of garlic, the anchovies, fresh basil and some salt and pepper. When ready, dress generously with the olive oil.

Before serving, slice the bread and rub all over with raw garlic, then drizzle with olive oil. Use your grill to toast on both sides or use a grill pan or ordinary non-stick frying pan over a high heat. Serve with the charred peppers.

Bruschetta of cannellini beans and ricotta

This next one is most unusual as it features cannellini beans on bread – think of it as a sort of Italian 'beans on toast', God forbid.

1 slice ciabatta bread per person
1 tin cannellini beans
Handful of black olives
1 clove of garlic
Extra-virgin olive oil
Sea salt
1 courgette or 1 bulb of fennel
1 small bunch of basil
1 tub of ricotta or 1 ball of mozzarella
3 ripe tomatoes, on the vine

Rub the bread all over, liberally, with olive oil, before grilling or toasting it. Then rub the bread with garlic.

Chop and de-seed the tomatoes and slice the courgette or fennel thinly, then rub with olive oil and chargrill.

Drain and rinse the beans and mix with the chopped garlic, basil, chopped black olives, black pepper and olive oil.

Spread the slice of toasted ciabatta with ricotta, sprinkle with sea salt and top with the bean mixture.

Arrange slices of charred courgette or fennel on top and, finally, top with the chopped tomato.

Bruschetta of goat's cheese with honey

Finally, here's quite an upmarket one, which you can bring out on the weekends – say for Sunday lunch – to impress. Despite being a bit fancy, it can bring old and somewhat tired ingredients back to life in a very real and meaningful way. While the honey and chilli are indispensable and bring their own little bit of magic, the rocket and the pine kernels are not essential if you don't have them and don't want to splash out.

But no, iceberg lettuce is not a reasonable substitute.

1 slice of stale bread per person
1 slice of goat's cheese per person
1 teaspoon of honey
Pinch of chilli flakes
1 sprig of thyme
Extra-virgin olive oil
1 clove of garlic
A few leaves of rocket
Pine kernels
Salt and pepper

Rub the bread all over with the garlic clove and moisten with olive oil on both sides.

Place the goat's cheese in a small oven dish and drizzle with olive oil. Swirl the honey around it, and sprinkle with chilli flakes and a little chopped thyme. Place the pine kernels around the cheese slice.

Place the cheese under a hot grill and allow to brown but not burn. Grill the bread on a grill pan or in a non-stick frying pan on both sides.

Assemble the dish by placing the grilled bread on a plate; top first with rocket and the toasted pine kernels, then slide the cheese on top, removing the outer rind.

Add a little crushed black pepper, if desired.

Croque-monsieur and croque-madame

Sometimes there's just nothing like sitting in a French café and enjoying a *croque-monsieur* washed down with some rough wine or a demi of beer. *Croque-monsieur* isn't just another 'ham and cheese toastie'; rather, it's an elaborate sandwich made with brioche, good-quality cheese and ham, and, in the original recipe, a béchamel sauce. These days, it's rarely made with brioche as per the orginal recipe; like crostini or bruschetta, it can be a great method for using up those (slightly) stale loaves, not forgetting any ham that might be heading for its sell-by date. For a while, I thought I'd gone off *croque-monsieur* but now, with the downturn, I'm all over them again. The *croque-monsieur* is a hundred years old in 2010; and was first mentioned by Proust in 1918 in the second volume of *Remembrance of Things Past*.

8 slices of bread, preferably a country loaf
160g Gruyère
4 slices of ham
Dijon mustard
Salt and pepper
Butter

At its most simple, all you have to do is toast the slices of bread on one side, then make the sandwich with the ham and plenty of cheese, plus a good layer of Dijon mustard, and either brown in a pan or under the grill. If you want to go the whole hog once you've got this far, make a thick béchamel as follows.

For the béchamel:

25g butter
30g flour
1 tablespoon flour
300ml milk

Begin by making a roux: add the flour to the melted butter and combine, allowing to cook, without burning, over a low heat. When this is done, add the hot milk slowly, whisking all the while. Allow to cook, whisking constantly. Season with salt, pepper and nutmeg.

Spread the thick béchamel on top of the sandwich, cover with a further layer of grated Gruyère (or Emmenthal) and place under the grill until bubbling. That's your *croque-monsieur*; if you fancy a fried egg too, cook one in the pan and place on top (giving you a *croque-madame*).

DESSERTS

Rhubarb and whiskey tart

I absolutely love rhubarb, and it remains a cheap and plentiful ingredient (when in season), suiting sweet desserts such as this, as well as partnering well with such lofty items as foie gras. It is famous for marrying sublimely with strawberries; if you don't fancy the whiskey, you could always add some of those to the mix.

For the pastry:

250g flour
125g butter
70g sugar
2 egg yolks
A little water and a pinch of salt

For the filling:

500g rhubarb
150g sugar
2 egg yolks
Small glass of Black Bush whiskey
150g crème fraiche
1 vanilla pod

Peel the rhubarb and cut it into rounds, Then place the chunks in a bowl with around 50g of sugar for an hour or two, to remove some of the excess water. Place in a fine sieve afterwards and press until the excess is eliminated.

Place the rhubarb in a saucepan and leave to cook very slowly with the split vanilla pod for around thirty minutes, stirring frequently.

During this time, make the sweet pastry. Beat the egg yolks with the sugar and a little water, then dice the butter and place it on top of the flour.

Use the fingers of both hands and mix the butter and flour together, rubbing gently, until the sand-like result falls through your fingers. In a bowl, incorporate the egg-and-sugar mix into this and mix gently, using a plastic spoon or other implement. Gently form a ball out of the mixture, adding a little more water if necessary.

Leave for around twenty minutes before rolling out and then cooking in an oven for about ten minutes at 180 degrees. (When placing in the oven, cover the pastry with greaseproof paper and cover with dry chickpeas or beans.)

When ready, remove the paper (and beans) and replace with the cooked rhubarb. Mix the remaining two egg yolks with 100g of sugar and all the crème fraiche, plus a generous splash of the whiskey, and pour this all over the rhubarb.

Return to the oven at 200 degrees for around another ten minutes or until the mix has browned.

Olive oil cake

Latterly I have discovered cakes such as this, made exclusively with olive oil, and marvelled at their flavour and lightness. I love to make this cake from time to time and watch people's faces as their demeanour turns from skepticism ('How can a cake be made without butter?') to unbridled joy. I've also tried to mess with it, adding ingredients and trying to improve upon it. Don't. There's no point.

I also think it needs precious little else to go with it – certainly not the likes of crème anglaise, which, to my mind, would sit uneasily with olive oil. If you must have something, try some fresh berries with honeyed fromage frais. That's the ticket.

180g flour
2 teaspoons of yeast or baking powder
Pinch of salt
225g sugar
3 eggs
Zest of 1 lemon
60ml milk
180ml extra-virgin olive oil
100g toasted chopped flaked almonds

Heat the oven to 180 degrees, and butter and flour a cake tin. Mix together the flour, baking powder and salt.

Using an electric whisk, beat the sugar, eggs and lemon zest together in a large bowl until the mixture becomes pale. Add the milk, followed by the olive oil. Now add the flour mixture to the egg mix and stir it in slowly.

Finally add the chopped almonds and transfer this dough to the cake tin or mould. Leave in the oven for at least forty minutes. Test by sticking a knife in: it should come out dry.

Leave to sit for twenty minutes before turning it out. Some punters thought I should shake icing sugar over the top. I don't.

Petits pots de chocolat (little pots of chocolate)

More olive oil! This time with chocolate – which gives a lightness and sheen to the confection.

120g good-quality chocolate, preferably dark
150ml milk
15ml cream (or yoghurt)
3 egg yolks
30g sugar
1 tablespoon olive oil

Begin by melting the chocolate in a bain-marie: fill a large receptacle with water, place on the heat and put a saucepan containing the chocolate in this water. When the chocolate has melted, place the saucepan on a very low heat and stir in the milk. If it's too thick, add a little more.

Meanwhile, whisk the egg yolks with the sugar, pour the chocolate mix on top and mix in.

Stir in the cream (or yoghurt). At this point, the chocolate mix could be flavoured further – with a tablespoon of Grand Marnier, for example.

Finally, stir in the olive oil, then transfer to small ramekins. Allow to cool before placing in the fridge for at least an hour.

Churros

Here it is again! More olive oil – this time from the country which is synonymous with it. As I may have mentioned one or twice already in these pages, I recently went to Spain for the first time and, while I'm sorry to bang on about it, the sight of a plaza on a sunny morning, festooned with churros-chompers, to a man, woman and child, is quite something. I indulged in this most wicked of breakfast items (or afternoon snack, or dessert, or whatever it is) rather too often. It's fun to make; you could supervise the kids doing it, and eat them all up together afterwards. Again, hot oil can be dangerous, so let the kids make the batter, and do the piping yourself.

Olive oil
Pinch of salt
1 teaspoon bicarbonate of soda
400g plain flour
Sugar and cinnamon

For the sauce:

120g dark chocolate
100ml milk
1 tablespoon cornflour
4 teaspoons sugar

Begin by sifting the flour and bicarbonate of soda into a bowl, then pour 400ml of boiling water in and whisk briskly to avoid lumps. When a smooth batter is obtained, leave it to rest for at least an hour.

Heat the oil and drop a little batter in to see if it sizzles, and therefore if the oil is hot enough. Using a cake decorator, pipe the batter into the oil in roughly 10cm strips and fry until golden brown.

When ready, place on absorbent kitchen roll and sprinkle with sugar and cinnamon if desired – though this is not traditional in Spain.

For the chocolate sauce:

Dissolve the chocolate in half the milk in a small pot until it is completely melted over a low heat.

Mix the cornflour into the rest of the milk and then add this to the melted chocolate along with the sugar.

Keep stirring until thickened.

When ready (after about five minutes), remove from the heat and whisk until smooth.

Polenta and almond cake

This is another type of Italian cake that I am very fond of. It's made essentially from polenta flour – the kind of cheap basic product that very much suits the philosophy of this book. Philosophy aside, however, it's a delicious cake and, like the olive oil cake, it goes a long way and also lasts a long time when kept in a cool place. Again, it's so soft and gentle on the tongue, and so full of flavour, that I don't feel it needs an accompaniment – not to mention the fact that we can't afford mascarpone.

225g polenta flour
Pinch of salt
Heaped teaspoon of baking powder
6 eggs
4 lemons, zested
The juice of one of those lemons
450g unsalted butter
450g sugar
450g ground almonds

Preheat the oven to 160 degrees.

Beat the butter and sugar together until the mixture begins to go pale. Now stir in the ground almonds. Continue to beat and add the eggs one at a time until they are fully absorbed. After this, add all the lemon zest, followed by the juice. When this is done (God will reward your beating in heaven), add the polenta flour and the baking powder. Continue to mix well – the mixture should be fairly thick yet loose – and add the pinch of salt.

Butter a mould or tart ring and dust it lightly with flour. Now add all the polenta mix – it will smell wonderful – and place it in the oven for around forty minutes, or until the cake is brown on top.

Apple and cranberry crumble

The auld crumble has fair stood the test of time, currently being one of the most popular desserts in France. Not content with nicking this most British of desserts, they are adapting the recipe for numerous savoury starters over there – a 'crumble of foie gras' being one of the most daring that I have seen. In Ireland, cranberries have become very popular, joining blueberries and pomegranates in the 'superfood' stakes, so here's an idea for an apple and cranberry crumble, should the notion take you.

About 4 apples (roughly 800g)
80g cranberries (fresh or frozen)
1 knob of butter
'Four-spice' mix
100g plain flour
100g chilled butter
80g demerara sugar or 'cassonade'
80g ground almonds

Wash and peel the apples, then cut them into small dice, throwing away the core.

Melt the butter in a pot and add the apples and cranberries, followed by the spice mix and a little water.

Mix well, then allow to simmer for around ten minutes.

In a salad bowl, mix the flour, sugar and ground almonds. Slowly add the chilled butter in small cubes, incorporating it quickly using your fingers. The mixture should take on a sandy texture.

Heat the oven to 200 degrees. Put the cranberry and apple mixture in a gratin dish and, using a tablespoon, put the crumble mixture on top without piling it up.

Smooth it out with the back of the spoon and place in the oven for around twenty minutes, or until the crumble is nicely browned.

Note that some authorities, fearful that the hot apple compote might render the crumble somewhat soggy, advise cooking the compote and the crumble separately and combining them at the last moment. This seems altogether sensible. You'll be needing cream, custard, ice cream or crème anglaise with that, of course; the recipes will follow.

Rhubarb crumble

The other great recipe for crumble is of course this one: rhubarb crumble. It really doesn't get much better than this.

12 sticks of rhubarb
A small glass of water
10 tablespoons caster sugar
100g butter
A pinch of ginger
110g demerara sugar
200g plain flour
150g hazelnuts

Preheat the oven to around 190 degrees.

Begin by trimming the rhubarb, cutting it into long sticks and putting it in an oven dish. Put all the caster sugar on it as well as the water, and put it in the oven to roast for about twelve minutes. Remove from the oven and prepare the crumble topping.

If you like the notion, you could always slice strawberries in with the rhubarb before applying the topping, as they go so well together.

To make the crumble, first chop all the hazelnuts, then simply mix the butter with the flour and sugar. When it resembles breadcrumbs, add the hazelnuts. Cover the rhubarb with this and leave to bake in the oven for about twenty-five to thirty minutes.

Chocolate madeleines

Madeleines are those lovely little funny-shaped buns that are golden and taste of vanilla. Here's a little departure from the norm where they are chocolate-flavoured and simply irresistible. Be careful not to eat the lot! This makes about twenty madeleines. You can make them in any mould for buns, of course, but if you can beg, borrow or steal the Madeleine moulds with the little indentation, then do so. Otherwise, don't worry your head about it.

3 eggs
100g plain flour
125g sugar
100g dark chocolate
115g unsalted butter
1 teaspoon baking powder

Make a 'double boiler' by placing a bowl over a pot of boiling water and melting the chocolate and butter together in it. Allow to cool. Then sift the flour and baking powder together. Beat the eggs in an electric mixer and slowly add the sugar. Now add the flour and baking powder manually and mix well with a wooden spoon. Add the chocolate-and-butter mixture and, when this is done, leave in the fridge for at least an hour before baking.

Fill the moulds with the mixture and cook in an oven preheated to 220 degrees for around seven minutes; reduce the heat to 190 degrees and allow to cook for four more minutes.

Walnut tart

I've made this a few times, and it is a very nice tart, if a trifle walnutty, so ya gots to likes walnuts. The filling is the best bit, so if you don't want too many walnuts, leave out the ones on top. Alternatively, leave them in, make it for special occasions, and serve small portions.

For the pastry:

125g plain flour
75g unsalted butter
25g granulated sugar
1 egg yolk
Salt
25ml water

For the filling:

500g walnuts
150ml cream
60g sugar
1 egg
1 vanilla pod

To garnish:

75g icing sugar
A small glass of rum
Whole walnuts for garnish

First of all, make the pastry by combining the flour, butter, granulated sugar, salt, water and egg yolk together until a ball forms. Leave to rest in a cool place for thirty minutes and then roll out and place in a buttered tart mould.

Pulse the walnuts in a mixer and then combine these with the cream, egg, sugar and vanilla pod. Mix very well, then pour onto the pastry. Bake in an oven preheated to 220 degrees for thirty minutes.

When the tart is cold, mix the icing sugar and rum together. Brush the tart with this and garnish with the walnuts, cut in half.

Honey-dipped briouats with almonds and dates

Here's an example of the heavenly little pastries that come from the countries of the Maghreb. I find them utterly irrestible, and run in the opposite direction if I see them; otherwise I will simply eat far too many. Nor will I tell a lie: I do not find them easy to make, being a clumsy beggar at best, but you might be more skilled in this department. There's nothing on earth more indulgent than these with some hot, sweet mint tea (though I've given up the sugar in that; miss it loads).

The orange-flower water is easy to pick up in either Asian shops or North African shops.

6 sheets of filo pastry
125g melted unsalted butter (for the pastry)
200g ground almonds
90g unsalted butter (for the paste)
60g icing sugar
Almond extract
Orange-flower water
1 jar of honey
4 Medjool dates

Using a heavy pan or saucepan, toast the ground almonds by stirring them constantly over a medium heat. Transfer to a bowl straight away.

Add the butter to the same pan and allow to melt; then add the icing sugar, a little almond extract and a tablespoon of the orange-flower water. Mix well until a paste forms. Cut the dates lengthwise, then chop them and add these too.

Brush strips of filo pastry with melted butter and then spoon in the almond-and-date paste. Fold over to form a triangle or cornet, and brush the outsides of the pastry with melted butter too. Continue doing this until the mix is finished.

Bake the *briouats* in the oven (preheated to 180 degrees) for about twenty to twenty-five minutes, until slightly golden.

During this time, combine the honey, a little water and two to three more tablespoons of the orange-flower water in a saucepan. Bring this mix to the boil and then leave to cool. Dip each pastry in this mix, removing with two forks, then transfer to a tray covered with baking paper and allow to cool.

Serve with freshly brewed mint tea. Go easy on the sugar.

Clafoutis

I'm glad to see that *clafoutis* has made such a come-back on restaurant menus. *Clafoutis* is a classic French dessert which is made on a batter but is exquisitely light and flavoursome. Cherries are traditional, though plums and apricots are also delicious. It seems that blueberries are what's hip to the groove right now, so let's use those.

250ml milk
80g flour
125g sugar
1 pinch of salt
4 eggs
Vanilla essence, or 25g of vanilla sugar
60g unsalted butter, in chilled cubes
250g fresh blueberries
150ml water and 50g caster sugar (to make syrup)

Begin by making the mix for the *clafoutis*, which is essentially the same as a crêpe batter.

Melt the butter in a saucepan and then leave to cool.

Put all the eggs in a bowl, then add the sugar and a pinch of salt. Mix well.

Then add the melted butter, followed by the milk.

Finally, sieve in the flour and mix slowly and well.

Meanwhile, make a syrup from the water and caster sugar and warm the blueberries in that for about five minutes (or, alternatively, just use the blueberries as they are).

Butter and flour the bottom and sides of a cake tin and arrange all the blueberries on the bottom. Then pour the *clafoutis* mix on top and bake in an oven preheated to 180 degrees for thirty to thirty-five minutes.

Salad of exotic fruits with ginger and vanilla

Mindful of the 'five a day' rule, it's always a good idea to get some fresh fruit into you. Here's an embarrassment of riches. I love the pink grapefruit in this – the star of the show.

1 small pink grapefruit
1 small fresh mango
1 banana
1 pineapple
1 small punnet of blueberries
1 vanilla pod, split
1 small piece of fresh ginger, grated
1 lime
1 lemon
100g light demerara sugar
A handful of fresh mint leaves, chopped finely (with a few leaves reserved for garnish)

Cut the vanilla pod in two lengthwise. Peel the ginger, then grate the whole piece finely. Grate the zest of both of the lime and the lemon and then squeeze out the juice.

Heat roughly 250ml of cold water with the vanilla, ginger, the zest of the lime and lemon plus all the sugar in a small saucepan. Bring to the boil, then add the juice from the citrus fruits and leave to cook until a syrup is formed.

Peel the grapefruit, segment it, removing all membrane, and cut the segments into small cubes.

Peel the mango and slice its flesh into large cubes.

Wash the blueberries under cold running water.

Peel the pineapple and cut it into rounds. Heat a grill pan and lightly grill the pineapple on both sides, marking it attractively.

In a large salad bowl, mix the grilled pineapple with the diced grapefruit, mango and blueberries. Stir in the chopped mint too.

Douse liberally with the ginger syrup and remove the vanilla pod.

Cover with clingfilm and leave to marinate for at least forty-five minutes, until it's well chilled.

When ready to serve, add the sliced banana and serve in individual bowls.

Crème anglaise

This is how to make the delicious sauce to accompany desserts.

> 7 egg yolks (keep the egg whites for Floating Islands
>   or one of those new-fangled egg-white omelettes
>   that give you an instant facelift – or so they say)
> 1 litre milk
> 5 tablespoons sugar
> 1 sachet vanilla sugar
> 1 teaspoon cornflour
> 1 tablespoon water

Put the egg yolks, water and both sugars into a mixing bowl and whisk the lot until the mixture becomes pale. Then mix in the cornflour.

Heat the milk in a saucepan, then pour it all over the egg mix and stir well. After that, empty it back into the saucepan and, using a wooden spoon, mix it well as it thickens, without letting it boil. When it begins to coat the back of the spoon, pour it through a wire mesh into another receptacle and allow to cool. Once it has cooled completely, store it in the fridge until needed.

Custard

That's the French version of custard. Now here's the English version.

6 egg yolks
50g caster sugar
250ml milk
250ml double cream
1 vanilla pod
2 tablespoons custard powder

In a similar manner to the preceding recipe, whisk the egg yolks, caster sugar and custard powder together in a bowl. Heat the milk and cream together, split the vanilla pod, scrape the seeds into the milk and then throw the pod in too. Allow to boil.

At this point, pour the hot milk into the egg mix and whisk together, then pour the lot back into the saucepan. Bring it back to the boil and use a spatula to stir, letting it cook for another few minutes over a medium heat to thicken. Goes really well with crumble.

EATING IN

Well, it has finally come to pass: eating in or staying in *is* now the new going out, as evidenced by half-empty restaurants the length and breadth of this country – and many other countries too. This doesn't mean that the partying needs to stop: staying in and eating in can be fun, and the well-prepared host or hostess need no longer be a slave to the stove in the twenty-first century, if he or she is organised. And that, dear impoverished gastronomes, is key. It astonishes me that some old clichés such as 'You're late. It's all in the oven, burnt' continue to be common currency when a little organisation, pre-cooking and thought as to menu can help avoid major disasters. No need either for meals and recipes to be plain or tasteless – as I hope this book has shown. We are reminded constantly of how the downturn is in fact a positive force, galvanising imagination coupled with parsimony; nowhere is this more apt than in cooking and domestic budgeting.

Here are a couple of tips and a few more simple recipes that will help have things ready, and also help compose a meal that is in harmony.

Being organised means making sure that your guests have a good time and are able to relax and leave your home feeling sated and happy. But it also means that you too have a good time, that your preparation is all done, and that all that remains for you to do is to assemble and expedite. *Boxed off*, as Irish chefs are wont to say. This leaves you free to attend to your guests and have (small) drinky-poos as well as imparting a feeling of well-being and relaxation if guests can see that you aren't flummoxed, constantly exiting to the kitchen or getting stressed.

Don't experiment with your guests. Cook what you know, or at least what you have successfully attempted previously. Nothing is worse than presenting a dish which you yourself are eating with a sinking feeling with each mouthful. Guests are not guinea pigs, and a 'wonderful new recipe' should be tried and tested before being foisted upon your best friends. Besides, gremlins can get into any recipe.

Keep the kitchen tidy and organised. This may seem obvious but it has many advantages. Quite apart from the ease with which you may assemble dishes, it also removes any hidden dangers lurking on the worktop, the hob and so on, where the handle of a pot could catch in your apron and come crashing to the floor, or an unwelcome ingredient may spill into your magnificent *salade folle*. If you do have several saucepans – a sauce, a vegetable or two, a puree – on the go at one time, then place an oven dish filled with water on top of your hob and place the saucepans into that. This keeps them together, reduces hazard points and, furthermore, keeps everything hot without further cooking or burning.

Make sure you have all the ingredients required for the dish. Before deciding to cook a given dish, shop for all the ingredients the day before and make sure that you can get those elusive Toulouse sausages or Merguez, that tube of harissa, the half-litre of groundnut oil that was there last week, or that Epoisses that Tesco used to stock (but no longer do thanks to the credit crunch).

Think about nibbles and your starter. To be honest, I don't normally suffer from main courses being burnt and/or overdone because I rarely start cooking them until everyone has arrived and all has been meticulously planned. I have something small ready to eat with an aperitif when they come, and have the starter ready. While they're eating the nibbles, I put on the main course. Increasingly, as the recession bites, I have turned my attention to stews, daubes, wet dishes, tagines and so forth – the stuff of this book – and so everything is ready, it merely has to be warmed, or kept warm, and served. Nevertheless, this still means that you should think carefully about your starter. Keep it simple. Keep it in tandem with your main course. If you have cooking to do for the main course, then have a simple starter plated that requires no cooking or, if you're making one of the wet dishes mentioned above, you can afford to do a little cooking – such as grilled goat's cheese – for a simple but elegant starter. The best thing, however, is to serve some class of salad as a starter, where all the work has been done long before anyone arrived – just remember to dress it at the last second – or a pâté or terrine, some recipes for which will be given later in this chapter.

Keep the main course simple. Don't over-elaborate. There is no need for ninety-six vegetables. One or two will do, especially if nutritious ingredients have been used in the previous course in, say, a salad. There is not always need for a sauce, either, unless the recipe specifically demands it. Meats can be simply grilled and served with condiments for a healthier but still tasty meal. By condiments, I mean the likes of mustard, sea salt, gherkins/cornichons, even Reggae Reggae Sauce (ha!) – but think too of the recipe given earlier for *gremolata*, that wonderful Italian boost to grilled foods such as white meats and fish. Healthy? You betcha.

Work backwards. Prepare the dessert first, then the main course and lastly the starter, which is usually something that needs to be as fresh as can be and singing on the plate. Clearly, if the dessert is something to be baked, then it will benefit from this approach. You may cook it the day before or on the morning of your dinner party but then it's done, and you can forget about it. Tidy away, then begin work on the main course.

Don't mix and match, and don't repeat ingredients. I hate magpie cuisine – you know, where you get spaghetti for a starter and then a tagine of partridge and prunes for a main. Yes, I am probably exaggerating, but you get my drift: keep it Italian or keep it French or keep it North African – you'll win. Look, say, at my various recipes for Maghrebi food: start off with those chickpeas, then follow with a tagine and serve one or two of those simple but glorious salads on the side. Be careful too to avoid needless repetition of ingredients. I mentioned earlier the goat's cheese starter – don't then have crostini with cheese as nibbles, and don't serve goat's cheese on your cheeseboard after the main course. In addition, this helps hammer home one of the many themes of this book: buy less, eat less, learn to think and eat differently.

Music. If you want music with your dinner, then gone are the days of blank silences while a CD is rummaged for or a dozen or more are lying around the floor afterwards, or skipping relentlessly as you're uncorking the next bottle. We all have iPods, right? Play the music back from the 'Pod or from the mother ship of the Mac or PC from which you installed the music in the first place, hooked up with a €2 mini-jack-to-phono cable attached to the auxiliary inputs of your hi-fi system. Create playlists of around an hour each: one each for aperitif, dinner, afterwards, for example, with music to match the conversation and the mood as food and drink are consumed.

Drink. You will of course need wine or beer, but there is no need to go to town on expensive or elusive bottles. Choose well. Seek out a fine Prosecco or a Crémant from the various regions of France if you want sparkling wine but cannot run to the heady prices of champagne. We know, of course, that they aren't as good, but they aren't unpleasant either, and we all continue to have a good time. Don't know Crémant? It's one of the cheaper delights of France, available as Crémant de Loire, Crémant de Bourgogne (avoid the red – it's foul) and Crémant d'Alsace. The latter is my favourite, chalk-dry, reasonably priced and with a lot of the elegance of champagne. As for red and white, it's clearly a matter of personal preferences, as palate and wallet will dictate, but be aware that the French are fighting back against some of the more garish aspects of New World wines. The lesser-known appellations are making a modestly priced splash in the arena; a good bet is usually one of the southern Provence/Occitania jobbies. Two of my favourite entry-level wines of recent years both hail from the Côte du Rhone: watch out for the marvellously titled 'Rock 'n' Rhone' and the equally hilarious 'Chat en Oeuf' (say it fast), whose label sports a cartoon egg and a cartoon cat perched on top.

Don't drink. Once upon a time, chefs in professional kitchens were given a soothing glass of wine, known as *la consolante*, in recompense for their toils, but Escoffier, in his wisdom, did away with all that and introduced the glass of barley sugar. His notions persist today in the pints of cold water or cold cordial which are regularly brought into the kitchen by front of house, to assuage parched throats. However, the notion of the domestic cook having a glass or two of wine as he or she soldiers on still prevails, in its Floydian flamboyance. Well, it's not a good idea: it doesn't make the food taste better, and it's potentially a recipe for disaster.

Dinner party dishes

Just so that your dinner party can go with a swing, here are some recipes for pâtés, rillettes and terrines that I particularly enjoy. These can be made in advance and then sliced and plated for your first course, taking a lot of pressure off you.

Rillettes of mackerel

Rillettes originate in Tours and Le Mans. They are similar to pâté and are cooked in a lot of fat. Recently, it has become popular to make a lighter version with fish; I salivate frequently at the thought of the rillettes of salmon in the Old Bank in Kilkenny. Here's an equally lovely recipe for rillettes of mackerel. (It would also suit salmon or fresh sardines.)

> *450g fresh mackerel*
> *2 shallots*
> *3 cloves of garlic*
> *A little unsalted butter*
> *Salt and black pepper*
> *A small tub of crème fraiche*
> *Herbs, such as dill, parsley or chervil*
> *Country bread, such as rye or sourdough*

Since this is a dinner party, we're allowing ourselves the use of crème fraiche. Plunge the mackerel into some simmering water. Should you have some vegetables to hand, you could aromatise the water by adding a little carrot, some celery, a couple of bay leaves and a splash of white wine.

When the mackerel is cooked (this should take less than five minutes), remove from the pot and allow to cool. When this is done, skin the fish (it should peel away easily) and make sure all bones are removed by running your hand over the fish.

Meanwhile, chop the shallots and garlic finely and sweat them in the butter over a very low heat. Crumble all the mackerel flesh and add this to the shallot mix after about four minutes' cooking and stir it all in. Then season and allow to simmer, before adding the crème fraiche (and no, pouring cream won't do). Leave to simmer for a further five minutes.

Leave to cool, then roughly mash it with a fork; add some herbs, preferably dill, but parsley will do. Check the seasoning and then cover and transfer to the fridge to set for the next twenty-four hours. When ready to serve, you can scoop it into a small pastry ring, pat down well, remove the ring and serve, garnished with the sourdough (toasted) and a few sprigs of dill. Should you feel it needs a little more, then by all means add a salad of rocket or a salad of mesclun (mixed leaves) simply dressed with olive oil and lemon juice.

Chicken liver mousse

Today's pâtés and mousses are rarely like the village ones of old; we buy them in supermarkets, all mass-produced in Belgium (except at Christmas time, when they are imported from France but are only slightly better), and really, all we need to do is make them ourselves. It isn't always practical – true *pâté de campagne* recipes involve such cuts as shoulder of veal, which is not readily available in this neck of the woods. Here is a simple recipe for a mousse, a perfect start to a simple but elegant meal and, again, one that can be prepared well in advance. This recipe will make plenty of mousse; it can be kept in the fridge for a couple of days, at least.

400g chicken livers
100g rindless fatty bacon, chopped finely
Small glass of port
1 bouquet garni
Small tub of pouring cream
8 black peppercorns
2 bay leaves
50g unsalted butter
3 cloves of garlic
1 small onion, chopped

Dash of cognac or Armagnac
Pinch of salt

Bring some water to the boil in a pot and add the peppercorns, celery and bay leaves. Allow to simmer. Trim the chicken livers if necessary; add them to the water and let them cook for about ten minutes. After this time, remove them and allow to cool.

Sweat the garlic and onion together with the bacon in a pan in the butter and cook for about four minutes, then transfer to a blender. Add to this the cooked livers, the cognac or Armagnac, the port and a pinch of salt. Blend all the ingredients together until a smooth consistency is achieved, then add about four tablespoons of cream. Transfer to individual ramekins and allow to set in the fridge.

Note that you could sauté the livers at the start rather than poaching them. You could also add green peppercorns to the mix at the end to give a delightful, pungent finish.

Chicken liver parfait

Chicken liver parfaits are all the rage these days.
Here's a quick-and-easy recipe for one.

175g unsalted butter
500g chicken livers
1 clove of garlic
Dash of dry sherry, splash of sherry vinegar
1 bay leaf
1 sprig of thyme, chopped
3 leaves of basil

Trim the chicken livers of all excess fat. Place a
little butter on a frying pan over a medium heat,
allow to foam and then add the livers. Fry them
for a couple of minutes until golden, then add the
garlic and allow to cook for another minute. Add
the chopped thyme and basil, and the sherry. Tilt
the pan and allow the sherry to catch fire, then
cook for another couple of minutes.

Place all the cooked ingredients, and the rest of
the butter, in a food processor and blend until
smooth. Season the mixture with good-quality salt
and black pepper before spooning it into a loaf
pan lined with clingfilm. Pat down flat, then leave
to chill in the fridge. When serving, slice with a
knife which has been dipped in boiling water.

Red pepper terrine

One for the vegetarian – and very like one prepared for me by a friend some years back in her
delightful garden in the sun – a fresh tomato and
goat's cheese terrine. I haven't got that recipe to
hand, but this is equally good.

1.5kg red peppers
1 teaspoon of gelatin or a leaf of gelatin
Cognac or Armagnac
Extra-virgin olive oil
Pinch of sugar
Handful of black peppercorns
250ml double cream or crème fraiche

Cut the peppers in half: remove the white stalks
on the inside and all the seeds. Then flatten the
slices and run a blade over the inside of the pepper, removing the membrane and revealing the
bright-red flesh underneath. When this has been
done, transfer the pepper pieces to a saucepan
containing water, a little sugar, a pinch of salt, a
dash of olive oil and some black peppercorns.
Bring to the boil, reduce the heat to simmer and
allow to cook for ten to fifteen minutes, until the
peppers soften. Pulse in a blender until you have
a purée, then push through a fine-mesh sieve.

Mix the purée with half the cream and whisk it in. Dissolve the gelatin in hot water and then add this to the mixture too. Whisk the other half of the cream until stiff and add this as well. Season with salt and pepper and add the cognac.

Now line a bread pan with foil and pour the pepper mixture into it. Place in the fridge for at least three hours until set. Serve with plenty of toasted sourdough bread and olive oil, and maybe a rocket salad.

A Final Word

The more visionary among us remind the rest of the population on the nightly news that the recession is in fact both a positive time and a time of opportunity, a climate in which new businesses can flourish and people can stop and think differently. Those businesses that thrive in these times are those which have managed to 'think differently' and to adapt and renew in these difficult circumstances.

We too must adapt in these unsure times. We owe it to ourselves to stay alive and healthy; despite the cutbacks, the dole queues, and our reduced spending power, it remains necessary to keep a roof over our heads and to eat well. We are revisiting time-honoured practices in shopping for, buying, preparing, cooking, eating and, above all, not wasting, food.

There's the rub. Twenty years of plenty, of

eating out three times a week, of buying ready-made foods and takeaways, have spoiled us and robbed us of a great deal of the knowledge and skills we need if we are to make do with little and to create delicious, nutritious meals from every-day, and perhaps meager, ingredients.

Even before the downturn arrived, I used to watch the Saturday-night ritual in my village, where Mercedes, BMWs and other fancy cars would pull up at one of the six awful Chinese takeaways I am ashamed to say that we have, some customers ordering a meal for six or more that probably cost ten times what it could have been produced for at home. While that was being 'pre-pared', the customer would pop into Xtravision next door and rent a couple of DVDs, so that all at home could sit in silence staring at the box, while thoughtlessly eating oversalted, oversweetened, over-glutamated, greasy, revolting, badly cooked rubbish made from low-quality ingredients and eaten with plastic spoons from foil tubs and brown paper bags. Unfortunately, this habit continues.

It's a frightening and sobering thought. So is the statistic that at least 20 percent of the food bought for use in the home ends up in the bin. Hopefully some of those excesses can be curbed, and the skills of budgeting and cooking solidly and sensibly will once more come to the fore.

We need to cook more often. In fact, we need to cook daily. No one expects city folk to live like country folk in France, Italy or Portugal, say, where a whole pig can be slaughtered and every part used to keep an entire family nourished and fed throughout a harsh winter. Why should we? We had buying power instead, a multiple-credit-card lifestyle where we paid others to do this for us. Or is that really what was happening? Was it not in fact that our demand for watered-down versions of the original were in fact destroying local cultures and customs, to the point where the traditions were dying in front of us? In our quest for exotic and foreign foods, encountered on holiday, that we wanted on our shelves all year round, we have now banished the seasons, abandoned taste and flavour in favour of uniformity and false colour, crippled local economies and businesses, and, of course, pushed prices up.

It isn't just monetary concerns that are raised but those of desire, passion and need. I remember as a child looking forward to each June and the strawberries I would eat with milk and a little sugar because we couldn't afford cream. My, what a taste, and what flavour. Now, every day I see strawberries in both my local fruit and vegetable shop and my local supermarket, and I don't think I've actually bought any for years. There is no desire or longing any more for these berries that grace most restaurants' dessert platters for the sake of colour – and taste nothing like those wonderful red fruits of childhood. It's the same for asparagus, cabbage, new potatoes (how come they're perennially new?) and most of our other daily products. About the only vegetable that I ever seem to see in season is curly kale, and even that is now washed, separated and bagged before hitting the supermarket shelves. Have we really become so lazy that we can't hold some kale leaves under cold running water?

In this part of the world, we have embraced the fast-food joints as our saviours, flocking to their salty, jammy fare, provided at perceived small cost, while in Spain the response to the recession is that they now flock instead to the *taperías*, the French to the little bistro on the corner, and the Italians to the beloved trattoria. The UK is seeing the continued rise of the 'all-you-can-eat' restaurant Taybarn (modelled on Golden Corral in the United States). Its slogan – 'Grab a plate, help yourself, help yourself again' – is the complete opposite of the examination of our alimentary habits that we need to make. Of course, there is no need not to continue to enjoy yourself – far from it – but we should be reflecting on our values and our appetites, not stuffing ourselves like pigs in a society already rife with obesity and other food-related health problems.

Yet, there is some hope. As mentioned earlier, sales of slow cookers have rocketed – showing that the public is rediscovering the art of stews, of braising, of long simmering. The idea is that you prepare a dish the night before, bung it in the oven and, when you arrive home from work, it's ready. Just like the old days. What we need to rediscover too are markets, bargains, cheap cuts, bartering, the pleasure of having simple and few ingredients, and the thrill of preparing a tasty dish and of breaking bread with each other.

It isn't all about dinner, either, or eating at home, but also about lunch at the office or your place of work. Instead of buying one of those calorie-laden sandwiches, all too often washed down with some ghastly sugary soft drink, prepare your lunch at home, or bring the ingredients for a good lunch, whether it's just a decent sandwich of your own confection or a few salads – and take some time for yourself. The cost of those freezing-cold, tasteless bought sandwiches adds up fast.

This good sense should apply across the board: compare prices, weigh your own fruit and vegetables, walk to the next shop to get a better bargain. At home, save stale bread and make croutons for salade niçoise, or the French onion soup in this book. Buy one of those breadboards with slats in them and keep the breadcrumbs that fall through. Toast them, put them in a foodsaver and mix them with dried herbs. You can use them in plenty of different dishes. Keep all vegetable trimmings for stock, potato skins for frying and serving as a garnish to meat or to eat with a dip – a dip that you've made yourself, of course. In fact, stop buying anything that you can make yourself, and watch the savings grow.

Gather up all your old bits of cheese and make a four-cheese sauce for macaroni. When cooking some of the recipes here, keep the fat that might solidify on top of a stock, or the oil used in the Spanish omelette – you can then use this to fry potatoes. By the same token, use less fat when frying meats: if you have a good non-stick pan, the lightest wipe with a piece of kitchen roll dipped in oil will suffice.

That's me finished giving out. I'm just sayin'. This book is not wearing any hair shirt, it's just making the case that, as a result of this crisis, we can go down another route, see things from another angle and continue to eat and live well by exploring tradition and applying a good dollop of common sense. I hope that you have enjoyed many of the recipes, because they are there principally for enjoyment – even though, at the same time, they will certainly help you save a few bob.